35.00

W9-AAW-856

AMERICAN RIGHTS

RIGHT TO VOTE

Deanne Durrett

Facts On File, Inc.

Right to Vote

Copyright © 2005 by Deanne Durrett
Maps and graphs copyright © 2005 by Facts On File, Inc.

All rights reserved. No part of this book may be reproduced or utilized in any
form or by any means, electronic or mechanical, including photocopying, recording, or by any information storage or retrieval systems, without permission in
writing from the publisher. For information contact:

Facts On File, Inc.
132 West 31st Street
New York NY 10001

Library of Congress Cataloging-in-Publication Data
Durrett, Deanne, 1940–
Right to vote / Deanne Durrett.
      p. cm.—(American rights)
Includes bibliographical references and index.
ISBN 0-8160-5661-7
1. Suffrage—United States—Juvenile literature. 2. Voting—United States—
Juvenile literature. I. Title. II. Series.
   JF831.D87 2005
   324.6'2'0973—dc22   2004022056

Facts On File books are available at special discounts when purchased in
bulk quantities for businesses, associations, institutions, or sales promotions.
Please call our Special Sales Department in New York at (212) 967-8800
or (800) 322-8755.

You can find Facts On File on the World Wide Web at http://www.factsonfile.com

Text design by Erika K. Arroyo
Cover design by Pehrsson Design
Maps and graphs by Dale Williams

Printed in the United States of America

VB FOF 10 9 8 7 6 5 4 3 2 1

This book is printed on acid-free paper.

Dedicated in loving memory to
my husband's brother
Buford Glenn Durrett
1930–2002

North Haven Memorial Library
North Haven, CT 06473

Contents

❦

Acknowledgments

The research and writing of *Right to Vote* spanned a year. During that time I received the support of many friends. I especially want to thank Diane Kennedy and Maritta Lipsit for long walks and good conversation over coffee at Joe's, and Pat and Dick Newell for more than 30 years of friendship.

I also want to thank election officials and poll workers who shared their experiences and provided information, including Karen S. Krauss, supervisor of elections, Sumter County, Florida, for taking time to chat with me about Florida's new voting equipment. And, writing friends who have volunteered as poll workers year after year: Carmen Bredeson, Marianne Dyson, and Lyn Seippel.

Last but not least I want to thank Shannon for posing for photos and Dan for critiquing every chapter at least twice and helping with the photos.

Introduction

Right to Vote, from 1789 to 2000

Sixty-nine electors from 11 states cast votes in the 1789 presidential election. There was no campaign, no primary election, no general election, and no popular vote (individual citizens' votes) was tallied. Yet the first president of the United States (George Washington) was elected exactly as specified in the U.S. Constitution.

More than 200 years later, 537 electors (one abstained) cast their votes in the 2000 presidential election. There was a campaign, primary election, and general election, and the popular vote was counted. The winner of the popular vote, however, was not the winner of the electoral vote. Several weeks later, the outcome of the presidential election was considered "too close to call" and in dispute. For the first time in history, a U.S. Supreme Court decision was required to ensure that a president of the United States was elected exactly as specified in the U.S. Constitution.

What happened between 1789 and 2000? The nation grew from 11 states to 50 and the population expanded from about 4 million to more than 275 million. The Electoral College grew from 69 to 538. In addition, the vote had been won for most American citizens age 18 and over.

The struggle for voting rights began with the Revolutionary War and American independence from Great Britain. The first U.S. voters were adult, white, male, property-owning citizens of the

United States. After the Civil War, black men were added to the electorate in 1865. During the next 100 years, women, American Indians, and young people 18 to 20 years old were granted the right to vote. In this process, the U.S. Constitution was amended eight times and blood was shed on Civil War battlegrounds and across the South in a long struggle for civil rights.

Winning the constitutional right to vote did not always guarantee the ability to exercise that right under state law. For instance, the southern black experience includes a 100-year struggle against state laws that denied blacks their constitutional right. Intimidation and vigilante tactics were used to keep blacks from voting. These laws and illegal tactics successfully disenfranchised southern blacks until Congress passed the 1965 Voting Rights Act. This legislation outlawed the discriminatory state laws and gave federal agents the authority to oversee voter registration and elections in each troubled southern county.

Today the right to vote is secure for most law-abiding, mentally competent adult citizens. Two generations of new voters have come of age since the last major voting rights battle. Many of the younger people, however, fail to recognize the importance of this precious right that protects all other rights. They do not vote.

The New Nation

Americans enjoy a government of the people, by the people, and for the people. These words seem to mean that everyone has the right to vote, and many people assume that this right is guaranteed in the Constitution. It is not. In the United States, much of the vote as it stands today was won through years of determination and courage that resulted in acts of Congress and amendments to the Constitution. The vote was won one segment of American society at a time—battle by battle, in a struggle that has lasted more than 200 years.

The struggle began with the colonists' dismay that the voting rights and representation that they had as English citizens disappeared when they arrived in America. With no representation in the British Parliament, the colonists could not defend themselves against unfair taxation. In time, they discovered that the right to vote helped protect all other rights. By 1774, the colonists had found that, not only were they taxed without representation, but that they had no right to due process (rules that must be followed to protect an individual's rights in legal matters). They were also subject to unreasonable search and seizure, and British troops could demand a place to live in their homes. When British oppression and taxation exceeded the colonists' tolerance, they were ready to fight for independence.

> "Let an Englishman go where he will, he carries as much of [English] law and liberty with him as the nature of things will bear."
>
> —Richard West, an official in the American colonies, in 1720

UNDER BRITISH RULE

Since England was more than 3,000 miles across the Atlantic Ocean from the American colonies, it seemed impractical, if not impossible, for the American colonists to send representatives to Parliament in London. Under British rule, each colony was governed by an assembly, a legislature-type body whose members were elected by the people. The highest officials, however, were appointed by the king of England but paid by each colony's assembly with tax money collected in the colony. This gave the colonists some power over the Crown-appointed officials who ruled them. For the first 150 years or so (from the first settlement at Jamestown in 1607 until after the French and Indian War in 1763), this arrangement did not matter much. The Crown and Parliament, occupied with events in Europe, paid little attention to governing the American colonies.

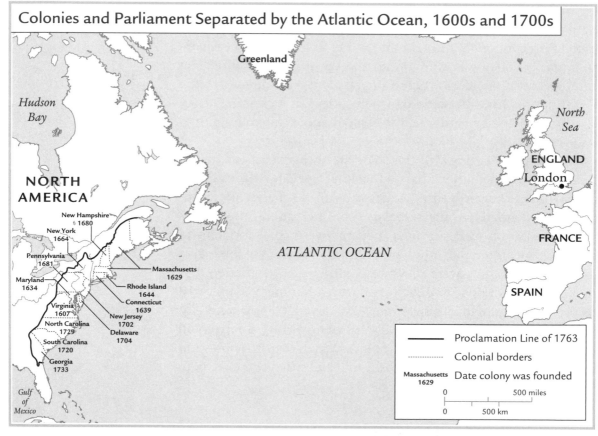

Colonies and Parliament Separated by the Atlantic Ocean, 1600s and 1700s

The thirteen colonies, stretched along the Atlantic coast on one side of the ocean, did not send representatives to the British Parliament, located on the other side of the ocean. The vast distance kept Parliament out of colonial business until after the French and Indian wars, when the colonies were recognized as a source of tax revenue.

GREAT BRITAIN

Scotland was formally united with England in 1707. England and Wales had formed a political alliance in 1536. With the addition of Scotland, these countries became known as Great Britain. (Ireland became a part of the United Kingdom of Great Britain [UK] in 1801.) These countries, along with the American colonies, were under the rule of the king of England (the Crown). And the military force that had been the English became known as the British.

WAR ON TWO FRONTS

The British colonies stretched along the Atlantic coast, and French territory in America lay west of the Allegheny Mountains, including the Mississippi and Ohio Valleys. As the population of the colonies grew, colonial settlement spread westward beyond the Alleghenies. As a result, war broke out between the French and British in America in 1754. American Indian tribes fought on both sides in this dispute, known in America as the French and Indian War. While fighting continued in America, Britain declared war on France in Europe in 1756. The Seven Years' War in Europe was actually an expansion of the French and Indian War in America. The wars ended in 1763 with France giving up most of its North American territory east of the Mississippi.

The victory left Great Britain with new American territory and a heavy financial burden. In addition, colonial settlement still approached a boundary with France and encroached on the Plains Indian territory. The people of England were already heavily taxed. They complained about the cost of protecting the American colonies from the French and hostile Indians. This brought the colonies, with their rich natural resources, suddenly into focus as a source of tax money.

THE TAX ACTS

To raise money, Parliament first passed the Sugar Act in 1764, which placed a tariff on molasses and refined sugar plus other imported goods. The Sugar Act stirred some resistance from the colonists and failed to produce the desired revenue.

> "If Taxes are laid upon us in any shape without our having a legal Representation where they are laid, are we not reduced from the Character of free Subjects to the miserable State of tributary Slaves?"
>
> —*Samuel Adams, May 1764*

In search of a better way to raise money, Parliament passed the Stamp Act in March 1765. This act was the first tax levied by the British on items produced within the colonies. The Stamp Act taxed almost every aspect of colonial business and everyday life, including commercial and legal documents, ship papers, licenses, newspapers, pamphlets, and playing cards.

British as well as American leaders saw the Stamp Act as the first step in establishing the right of Parliament to levy a direct tax upon the colonies.

STAMP ACT CONGRESS

Taxation without representation stirred the wrath of the colonists, and on October 7, 1765, representatives from nine colonies met in New York to discuss the matter. They were known as the Stamp Act Congress. These men compiled a formal list of grievances concerning the "present and impending misfortunes of the British colonies." They adopted Resolutions of the Stamp Act Congress on October 19, 1765, and prepared a formal document to send to George III, the king of England. These resolutions stated "[t]hat it is inseparably essential to the freedom of a people, and the undoubted right of Englishmen, that no taxes be imposed on them, but with their own consent, given personally, or by their representatives." They demanded the repeal of the unconstitutional taxes and threatened a boycott of British goods in the colonies. The Stamp Act, however, would take effect on November 1, 1765, long before a response from the king could be expected to arrive from England by ship.

VIGILANTE TACTICS

Unwilling to accept any British tax, a group of men in Boston called the Loyal Nine took measures to prevent the sale of tax stamps. They used mob violence and vigilante tactics to intimidate the newly appointed tax commissioner.

Other groups known as the Sons of Liberty formed throughout the colonies and used similar tactics against other stamp commissioners. This intimidation worked so well that all the appointed commissioners resigned before they sold any stamps. Unable to enforce the tax and fearing the boycott, Parliament repealed the Stamp Act in March 1766.

THE TOWNSHEND ACTS

Parliament and the Crown failed to realize the strength of the colonists' resentment toward taxation without representation. They tried another approach. In 1767, the Townshend Acts placed import duties on glass, lead, paint, paper, and tea. Attempting to enforce the taxation, Parliament further eroded the colonists' rights

With the Boston Tea Party depicted in the background, this political cartoon expresses the attitude of many Patriots who often gathered under a "Liberty Tree" to discuss British taxation. As shown here, they also tar and feathered tax collectors (excisemen). *(Library of Congress, Prints and Photographs Division [LC-USZ62-33262])*

LIBERTY TREE

Boston's Loyal Nine held their first secret meeting in the shadow of a huge tree (about 120 years old at the time). The next morning, British tax officials found replicas of themselves hung in effigy from its branches. This tree, standing in a public square at the intersection of Essex Street and Orange Street in colonial Boston, became the original Liberty Tree. As other Patriot groups formed throughout the colonies, the organization became known as the Sons of Liberty, and every group had its own liberty tree. The liberty tree became an American symbol that adorned many flags during this time.

by authorizing unlimited search warrants called writs of assistance. They also strengthened the Quartering Act of 1765, which required that the colonists provide food, drink, and lodging for British troops and their horses.

In response to these acts, the Sons of Liberty took their vigilante tactics a step further and began tar and feathering tax agents. This painful and humiliating act involved smearing the victim with hot tar and plastering him with feathers. Removing the tar called for a stiff scrub brush and smelly turpentine. Again, the intimidation worked. No one was willing to serve as tax agent, and these import taxes were repealed.

TEA TAX

Parliament passed a new tea act in 1773. This act lowered the price of tea sold in the colonies by Britain's East India Company. Along with taxation, the Tea Act was a plan to monopolize the colonial tea market and save Britain's failing East India Company from financial ruin. The attractive lower price, however, included a small tax, three pence per pound. Strongly opposed to any tax levied by Parliament, the colonists refused to buy the bargain-priced tea.

The Sons of Liberty used vigilante intimidation tactics against the agents of the East India Company in ports along the Atlantic coast. As a result, the agents in all ports except Boston resigned.

Ships that could not dock returned to England with a full cargo. Three ships, however, continued on to Boston and reached port on November 27, 1773. The Sons of Liberty stood guard on the dock and prevented the unloading of the ships. The ships remained in the harbor, and the standoff continued until December 16.

That night, while thousands of Bostonians crowded the streets to watch, Samuel Adams, John Hancock, and Paul Revere led the Sons of Liberty aboard the ships to dump tea valued at 9,659 pounds sterling into Boston Harbor. Angered by what is now known as the Boston Tea Party, King George III retaliated with the Coercive Acts.

In England, they were called the Coercive Acts, intended to force (coerce) the colonists to submit to British rule. In the colonies, however, these were known as the Intolerable Acts. The colonists' desire for representation in government had been further denied, and British rule now extended into the American home. The colonists would not accept this oppression and continuing loss of freedom. Massachusetts Institute of Technology (MIT) professor and history scholar Pauline Maier describes the colonists as "people

---

COERCIVE ACTS

- **Port Act:** Closed Boston Harbor to all shipping until Boston paid the East India Company for the tea destroyed during the Boston Tea Party.
- **Massachusetts Government Act:** Annulled (canceled) the Massachusetts colonial charter and placed the governance of Massachusetts completely under the Crown. It abolished town meetings and replaced all elected officials with royal appointments.
- **Justice Act:** Protected the royal officials in Massachusetts from legal action against them for acts involving riot suppression or revenue collection. All such cases would be transferred to England.
- **Quartering Act:** Continued the quartering (lodging) of British troops in all colonies at the colonists' expense and included troop lodging in private homes as well as public and unoccupied buildings.

with an enormous sensitivity to the dangers of power" and explains that if they "conceded the right to Parliament to tax and if there was no check on it . . . it could go on indefinitely. . . . The power to tax was the power to destroy." Motivated by this threat to liberty and determined to have a vote in the legislative body that levied tax on them, a group of colonial activists called a secret meeting. They kept this meeting secret because what these activists were about to do was an act of treason against the Crown.

THE FIRST CONTINENTAL CONGRESS

On September 5, 1774, 56 delegates representing 12 American colonies gathered in Carpenter's Hall in Philadelphia. (Georgia did not send delegates to this intercolonial meeting.) Until this time, each colony had stood alone. Now the colonies were united against their common enemies, British oppression and taxation, in the First Continental Congress.

Among those men gathered in Carpenter's Hall, several would rise to fame as "founding fathers" of the new nation. These included John Adams, Samuel Adams, Robert Trent Paine, John Jay, Richard Henry Lee, Benjamin Harrison, Patrick Henry, and George Washington.

The Congress wanted to present a united effort to assert their rights as Englishmen guaranteed by the British Bill of Rights. They did not wish to break with England and did not yet seek independence. They wanted to have a vote in the body that taxed and governed them.

Members of the First Continental Congress composed a carefully worded petition that expressed loyalty to the Crown while presenting a list of grievances and violations of their right to representation. They asked that the Intolerable Acts be rescinded (canceled). In further response to the Intolerable Acts, the Congress also passed an intercolonial resolution calling for a boycott of British goods throughout the colonies. They formed an organization called The Association to enforce the boycott. The First Continental Congress adjourned on October 26, 1774, but agreed to meet again on May 10, 1775, if Parliament did not repeal the Intolerable Acts.

"The distinctions between Pennsylvanians, New Yorkers, and New Englanders are no more. I am not a Virginian but an American."

—*Patrick Henry, delegate from Virginia to the First Continental Congress*

GRASSROOTS MOVEMENT

While awaiting the king's response, The Association worked to stir resentment against the British throughout the colonies. Leaders of the grassroots movement made speeches in the colonial legislatures to gain support for a military stand against Britain if King George rejected the petition. Patrick Henry made such a speech before the Virginia House of Burgesses on March 23, 1775. He presented a resolution to organize a Virginia militia and ready the colony for possible war with Britain. The last few words of his speech would echo through history: "I know not what course others may take; but as for me, give me liberty or give me death!" Speeches such as this one gained support for the Patriots and weakened respect for the Crown-appointed government. The Intolerable Acts remained in effect, and sentiment for American independence gained strength each day.

KING GEORGE III RESPONDS

Meanwhile, in England, King George III was in no mood to respond to any demands from the rebellious colonies. In response to news of unrest in America, he declared, "The colonies are in open and avowed rebellion. The die is now cast. The colonies must either submit or triumph." In a final response to the unrest in the colonies, King George ordered General Thomas Gage, the British colonial governor and general in America, to take decisive action to end the rebellion in the colonies. British troops set out on a march from Boston to Concord by way of Lexington on April 18, 1775. They planned to destroy the colonial arms storehouse at Concord. King George expected the colonists to submit as soon as British troops made a show of force.

FROM LEXINGTON TO YORKTOWN

As the British marched into Lexington at about dawn on April 19, they found American minutemen drilling on the village green. (These fighting men were called minutemen because they could be ready for battle with a minute's notice.) When ordered by the British to disperse, the vastly outnumbered minutemen held their ranks until ordered otherwise by militia commander Captain John Parker. As they began to disperse, one shot was heard, followed by a volley of British fire. And thus, no one can be certain who fired

The painting in this photo depicts members of the Second Continental Congress as they voted to declare American independence from Great Britain. *(National Archives Still Picture Records [MNDNS-148-CCD-35])*

what is known as "the shot heard 'round the world" that began the Revolutionary War in America.

The Second Continental Congress became the governing body that united the colonies during the war years. It established the Continental army with General George Washington as commander in chief. While the battle raged, this congress wrote the Declaration of Independence, and on July 4, 1776, the United States formally declared independence from Great Britain. Victory, however, would not be theirs until almost 8,000 British troops laid down their arms in surrender at Yorktown, Virginia, on October 17, 1781.

With the victory won, the Continental Congress would need to find a way to unite 13 unique and individual colonies into one nation.

ARTICLES OF CONFEDERATION

During the Revolutionary years, the colonies united under a loosely formed government described as "a firm league of friendship" by the Continental Congress in Article III of the Articles of Confederation. This document, however, failed to give the governing body the necessary authority and power. Any vote in the Congress required a quorum (minimum number) of nine states, yet Congress did not have the power to demand the attendance of any delegate. This presented a significant problem when the Treaty of Paris (formally ending the Revolutionary War) came before Congress for ratification in November 1783. Weeks passed before a quorum could be assembled. Congress finally ratified the treaty on January 14, 1784.

In addition to the difficulty in reaching a quorum, Congress did not have the authority to raise funds, regulate trade, or conduct foreign policy. George Washington complained that the government was "little more than a shadow without substance." On February 21, 1787, the Continental Congress began the process that would attempt to strengthen the government by revising the Articles of Confederation. It resolved to hold a constitutional convention with delegates representing each state. This convention met on May 14, 1787, in the Pennsylvania State House (now known as Independence Hall), and reached a quorum on May 25, 1787.

CONSTITUTIONAL CONVENTION

The first attempts at revising the Articles of Confederation brought lengthy discussions and heated debates. By the middle of June, members of the convention decided to draft an entirely new constitution.

Hot disputes erupted between those who wanted the states united as one nation under a strong federal government and those who wanted independent sovereign states joined in a confederation. The southern states feared federal meddling in the slave trade, and the northern states worried about stricter navigation laws. A matter of great concern to all was who would have how many votes in Congress. The small states wanted equal representation, while the large states wanted representation based solely on population. In addition, they had to decide who (president or king) would lead the new nation and how he (without question it would be a man) would be selected. The whole frame of the government (along with a provision for amendment) of the United States was constructed in summer 1787, and it has stood the test of time remarkably well.

"The Eyes of the United States are turned upon this Assembly and their Expectations raise to a very anxious Degree. May God Grant that we may be able to gratify them, by establishing a wise and just Government."

—*Virginian George Mason, in a May 1787 letter to his son as the delegates gathered at the Constitutional Convention*

New Hampshire became the ninth state to ratify (approve) the Constitution on June 21, 1788. The two largest states ratified it in the next five days—Virginia on June 25 and New York on June 26. With the Constitution ratified by 11 states (nine were required), Congress appointed a committee to put the Constitution into operation.

ELECTING THE PRESIDENT

On September 13, 1788, Congress passed a resolution setting the process in motion for the election of the first president of the

George Washington served as commander in chief of the Continental army before he became the first president of the United States. Washington was elected with a unanimous vote, winning all 69 electoral votes that were cast. *(Library of Congress, Prints and Photographs Division [LC-USZ62-117116])*

United States. The first Wednesday of the following January would be the date for states to select their presidential electors (delegates to the electoral college). Each state was allowed electors equal to the number of the state's senators and representatives. The methods for choosing the electors, however, was left to the individual states.

By Wednesday, January 7, 1789, the New York legislature had not passed an election act. Therefore, that state had no way to choose its electors and lost its eight votes. On February 4, 1789 (the date set to cast the electoral votes), three electors failed to vote, one from Virginia and two from Maryland. When the First Congress of the United States convened on March 4, 1789, the votes were counted. Sixty-nine electors had cast 69 votes, unanimously electing George Washington president of the United States.

The U.S. Constitution established the voting procedure for the legislative body of the federal government. The citizens' vote was not addressed in the Constitution or the Bill of Rights. Who could vote and how the vote would be cast in future elections remained a decision for each state. In years to come, who should vote and who should not would bring controversy, unrest, and bloodshed.

2

~⚮~

African Americans
Win the Vote

Before the nation was born, some people thought it strange that Americans had enormous concern for their own rights while denying those same rights to others. For example, Abigail Adams wrote to her husband, John, while he was attending the Continental Congress in Philadelphia. She reminded John Adams of five petitions delivered to Governor Thomas Hutchinson of Massachusetts calling attention to the slaves' plight. She expressed her concern about seeking freedom for some people while oppressing others. She wrote that "it always appeared a most iniquitous [unjust] scheme to me to fight ourselves for what we are daily robbing and plundering from those who have as good a right to freedom as we have."

Some colonial leaders also noticed the irony in the Patriots' demands for liberty and the acceptance of slavery throughout the colonies. James Otis, one of the Sons of Liberty and a member of the Stamp Act Congress, called the slave trade "the most shocking violation of the law of nature." Still, after independence was won, politics and compromise played a role in the writing of the Constitution. Otherwise, some of the nine states necessary to ratify the Constitution would have refused. Consequently, slavery was accepted and the rights of women were ignored. When the U.S. Constitution was ratified, about half the citizens (women) could not vote and a half-million people living in the United States (African slaves) were declared noncitizens. (At this time, American Indians were not citizens.)

PRINCE HALL
Free Black Activist

Prince Hall received his certificate of manumission (release from slavery) in 1770. Hall, listed in Massachusetts records as a voter and taxpayer, owned a small house and leather workshop in Boston. He founded the African Lodge of the Honorable Society of Free and Accepted Masons of Boston. This is the first American society devoted to social, political, and economic improvement for blacks. Hall used his position as "Worshipful Master" of the black Masons to speak out against slavery and the denial of black rights.

ABOLITION MOVEMENT

As long as the thirteen colonies had remained separate, each set its own policy toward slavery. The economy of the tobacco- and cotton-growing colonies in the South was dependent on slave labor. In the industrial northern colonies, however, slaves were usually household servants. So slavery divided the North and South from the beginning. While Southerners held fast to slave labor, many Northerners freed their slaves. Many of those with strong antislavery feelings joined in organizing the abolition movement. This included free blacks as well as whites.

Many women, seizing their only opportunity to participate in politics, joined their husbands in the expanding antislavery movement. Several of these women would later lead in the fight for women's suffrage. Many of them made speeches against slavery, although women were not generally accepted in the political arena and, in fact, were customarily discouraged from speaking in public. These women included Ida B. Wells-Barnett, Elizabeth Cady Stanton, and Lucretia Mott. They were sincere in their desire to abolish slavery and gain freedom and voting rights for blacks. They believed that women would be allowed to vote when African slaves gained freedom, citizenship, and suffrage.

THE ROAD TO EMANCIPATION

Northern states began abolishing slavery during the Revolutionary War. Vermont abolished slavery in 1777, and Pennsylvania followed in 1780. By 1808, antislavery states had enough influence in Congress to ban the importation of African slaves. Enforcing the law along the vast U.S. coastline proved to be impossible with the small U.S. naval force. Smuggling of African slaves flourished, and new arrivals continued to be sold in southern slave auctions. The southern states saw the federal ban on imported slaves as a threat to their economy, which was dependent on slave labor. The issue began to create hostility.

By 1820, there were 22 states—11 free states and 11 slave states. As more territories applied for statehood, legislators fought to keep a balance in the Senate between those favoring and those opposing slavery. Each time a free state was admitted (sending two anti-

---

DRED SCOTT V. SANFORD

Dred Scott, a slave, filed suit against his owner to obtain freedom for himself, his wife, and their children in 1846. Dred Scott claimed to be a citizen of the state of Missouri and assumed his rights as a citizen included the right to sue in federal court. When the case reached the U.S. Supreme Court, the Court examined African-American citizenship and considered the constitutionality of the Missouri Compromise and federal involvement in controlling slavery within territory gained in the Louisiana Purchase and new states.

On March 6, 1857, the Supreme Court ruled in a 7-2 decision that, according to the U.S. Constitution, a slave of African descent could not be a citizen of the United States and therefore could not file a suit in federal court. The Court also declared that the Missouri Compromise of 1820 was unconstitutional and determined that the federal government had no right to prohibit slavery in new territories. In addition, the Court ruled that slaves were property. When a slave owner took a slave into a free state or territory, the slave remained his property and could not claim freedom.

slavery senators to the Senate), a slave state was admitted (sending two proslavery senators to the Senate). For example, as part of the 1820 Missouri Compromise, Maine was admitted as a free state and Missouri as a slave state. The Missouri Compromise eliminated slavery in the territory acquired in the Louisiana Purchase north of longitude 36°30' (the southern border of Missouri). More than 25 years later, the U.S. Supreme Court ruled in the *Dred Scott* decision that the Missouri Compromise was unconstitutional.

This decision increased the antislavery outcry in the North. At the same time, it was received enthusiastically in the South, where slave labor created a prosperous economy. Strong feelings raged on both sides of this issue. The *Dred Scott* decision fanned the flames of these emotions and brought the United States to the brink of civil war.

NORTH AND SOUTH

The last slave ship docking in the United States unloaded its cargo in Mobile Bay, Alabama, in 1859, and Abraham Lincoln won the presidency in 1860, the first Republican to do so. By this time, geographical lines had been drawn between northern free states and southern slave states. Eleven southern states decided to secede (formally withdraw) from the Union and form the Confederacy.

During the Civil War years, from 1861 to 1865, the South fought to keep its prosperity and aristocratic (upper-class) lifestyle while the North fought to preserve the Union. The underlying cause, however, was slavery.

While the Civil War raged, President Lincoln issued the Emancipation Proclamation on January 1, 1863.

Some people link the Emancipation Proclamation to the end of slavery. The document, however, did not legally free one slave, grant citizenship, or guarantee anyone the right to vote. This presidential proclamation applied only to states that had seceded from the Union. These states had formed their own government in the Confederacy. Lincoln was not their president.

"That on the first day of January, in the year of our Lord one thousand eight hundred and sixty-three, all persons held as slaves within any State or designated part of a State, the people whereof shall then be in rebellion against the United States, shall be then, thenceforward, and forever free . . . and that the Executive government of the United States, including the military and naval authorities thereof, will recognize and maintain the freedom of said persons."

—*President Abraham Lincoln, Emancipation Proclamation, January 1, 1863*

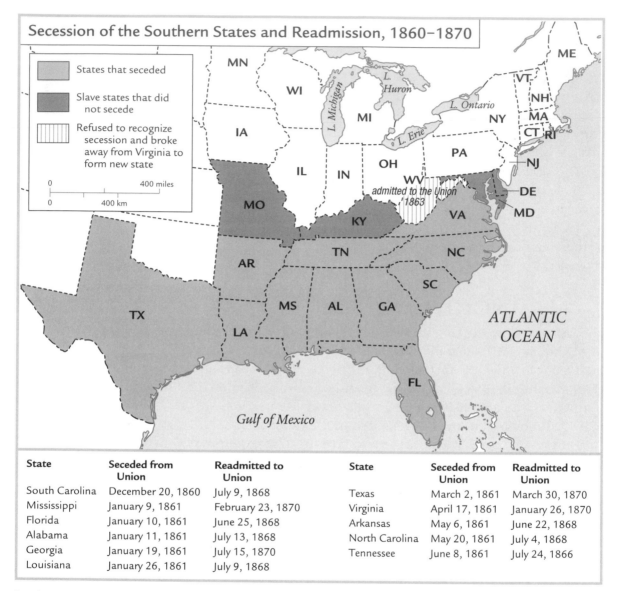

Secession of the Southern States and Readmission, 1860–1870

States that seceded

Slave states that did not secede

Refused to recognize secession and broke away from Virginia to form new state

State	Seceded from Union	Readmitted to Union	State	Seceded from Union	Readmitted to Union
South Carolina	December 20, 1860	July 9, 1868	Texas	March 2, 1861	March 30, 1870
Mississippi	January 9, 1861	February 23, 1870	Virginia	April 17, 1861	January 26, 1870
Florida	January 10, 1861	June 25, 1868	Arkansas	May 6, 1861	June 22, 1868
Alabama	January 11, 1861	July 13, 1868	North Carolina	May 20, 1861	July 4, 1868
Georgia	January 19, 1861	July 15, 1870	Tennessee	June 8, 1861	July 24, 1866
Louisiana	January 26, 1861	July 9, 1868			

Southern states seceded from the Union one by one as they joined the Confederacy. After the Civil War, they rejoined the Union, one by one. Four other slave states remained with the Union.

Consequently, they did not consider themselves bound by Lincoln's proclamation. As the Union armies advanced into the South, the territory that came under their control became free territory. As a result of Lincoln's proclamation, the slaves freed by advancing Union troops were able to join the Union army or navy. By the end of the war, almost 200,000 blacks had joined the Union forces and participated in liberating their people.

THE AMENDMENTS

Constitutional changes would be necessary to abolish slavery and give African Americans citizenship with the right to vote. These changes would be made in the Thirteenth, Fourteenth, and Fifteenth Amendments, passed by Congress and ratified by the states in the five years immediately following the war (1865–70).

The Thirteenth Amendment abolished slavery; the Fourteenth Amendment gave the freed slaves citizenship and gave all adult male citizens the right to vote. The Fifteenth Amendment prohibited

President Abraham Lincoln discussed the Emancipation Proclamation with his cabinet on September 22, 1862, but waited until January 1, 1863, to issue the Proclamation. *(Library of Congress, Print and Photographs Division [LC-USZ62-7275])*

states from passing laws that denied African-American men the right to vote.

Clear as the meaning of these amendments may seem, in the following years the U.S. Supreme Court was asked to determine exactly who was given what rights under these amendments. Unfortunately, these amendments and resulting Supreme Court decisions did not eliminate racism or prevent prejudice. Prejudiced people continued violating and suppressing the constitutional rights of African Americans.

RECONSTRUCTION PERIOD

The Civil War left the Union a fractured nation that would take 12 years to rebuild. The years 1865 through 1877 are known as the Reconstruction period. During this time, the 11 states that had formed the Confederacy came under Union military rule until state governments could be reestablished. To meet the requirements for readmission into the Union, each secessionist state's constitution was rewritten to abolish slavery and affirm loyalty to the Union. Each state was also required to ratify the Fourteenth Amendment. During this time, Confederate men (who had rebelled against the Union) lost their right to vote. Consequently, black male voters suddenly held a majority in these southern states. Aided by northern Republicans, some blacks were elected to local and state offices.

In response, strongly prejudiced Southerners formed white supremacy organizations such as the Ku Klux Klan. The Ku Klux Klan used violence and vigilante tactics to keep blacks from voting or running for office.

"Congress passed a law that every white man in the South must take an oath whether he had held any state or Federal office before the war and if later he had aided the cause of the Confederacy. Those who had done these things were disqualified as voters in the elections . . . [this placed] the government in the hand of what we called the 'carpetbaggers' [white] men from the North and the freed Negroes."

—*Sarah Ann Pringle,*
recalling life in Texas
after the Civil War,
ca. 1936–1940

STATE LAWS

When the southern states reentered the Union, they wanted to put whites back in office and recover control of the state governments. They found creative ways to disenfranchise (deprive of the right to vote) African Americans. For example, in 1889, North Carolina voter registration required detailed information about a voter's age and birthplace. Most people born in slavery did not have this information and could not meet the voting requirements.

Other disenfranchisement tactics included literacy tests, such as reading and explaining a section of the state's constitution.

Some states made it difficult for an illiterate person to mark the ballot. For example, Virginia's 1894 Walton Act required a ballot that listed candidates' names, but no symbols or political parties. The voter marked the ballot by scratching (crossing out) the names of the candidates he did not want to elect. A name was considered unscratched if the line did not extend three-quarters of the length of the printed name. An illiterate person was likely to leave too many names unscratched. As a result, the vote would not be counted, and the voter would be denied the right to vote.

POLL TAX

The poll tax proved to be a long-lasting and effective method to disenfranchise African Americans. The southern states levied poll taxes ranging from one to two dollars per person on the adult citizens of the state. Most states required payment of the tax in the election year plus the two preceding years. This meant that a person would have to pay three to six dollars to vote for the first time. This amount seems like a small sum by today's standards, but in the early 1900s, many poor families lived on $100 (or less) per year. Literacy tests and the poll tax denied the vote to many poor, illiterate men, whites as well as blacks.

To avoid disenfranchising white voters, new laws were written that allowed men to vote if their grandfather had been eligible to vote. Most states also allowed men to vote if they had served in the Confederate army or if their father had served.

VIGILANTE JUSTICE

Without the right to vote, African Americans could not elect candidates who would represent their interests. Consequently, they had no political voice in state and federal government. This left them at the mercy of law enforcement officials who were elected by and accountable to white voters. Most of these elected officials ignored the African-American citizen's right to fair trial and due process. As a result, many innocent African Americans become the victims of vigilante justice carried out by the Ku Klux Klan and lynch mobs. According to Library of Congress, 500 blacks were known to be lynched in the last five years of the 1800s (1895–99). The number of lynchings per year began to decrease slowly after

"... the convention has the fixed and unalterable [unchangeable] intention of enacting a clause which will ... forever remove the negro as a factor in our political affairs and give to the white people of this Commonwealth the conduct and control of the destinies which they have the right to shape and determine."

—Honorable J. Taylor Ellyson, chairman of the Virginia Democratic Committee, 1901

the National Association for the Advancement of Colored People (NAACP) drew attention to these crimes and began to fight for African-American civil rights.

CIVIL RIGHTS MOVEMENT

The NAACP is the oldest, largest, and strongest civil rights organization in the United States. It was organized in 1909 in New York City. The original founders include Mary White Ovington, Henry Moscowitz, Oswald Garrison Villiard, William English Walling, Ida Wells-Barnett, and W. E. B. DuBois. These black and white activists worked to fight social injustice through the courts.

In an early NAACP case, *Guinn v. United States,* the U.S. Supreme Court declared that Oklahoma's grandfather clause (a person could vote if he could prove that his grandfather had voted) was unconstitutional because it violated the Fifteenth Amendment. For the next 50 years, the NAACP worked through the courts to end segregation, unfair housing practices, and voter intimidation. Still, most of the disenfranchisement laws remained in place blocking African Americans from the polls.

On December 1, 1955, Rosa Parks refused to give up her seat in the "black section" of the bus to a white man. This violated Alabama segregation laws, and Rosa Parks was arrested and fined $14. This incident brought Martin Luther King, Jr., to the scene and hurled the Civil Rights movement into a nonviolent pursuit of social change. The NAACP continued the fight for civil rights in the courts while King took the fight for voting rights into southern cities and towns. Freedom marchers and riders began registering black voters. Even so, as long as the poll tax and other discriminating laws remained in force, most blacks were denied the vote.

TWENTY-FOURTH AMENDMENT

The effort to abolish the poll tax dates back to 1939. By this time, women had the right to vote, but most women in the South (black and white) could not afford to pay the poll tax. Civil rights activist Virginia Durr wrote in her autobiography that "If a poor tenant farmer had scraped up a dollar and a half to pay his poll tax, he sure . . . wasn't going to pay a dollar and a half for his wife. And women themselves never had any money." The National Committee to Abolish the Poll Tax (NCAPT) was formed in 1941. Several other groups, including labor unions, churches, and civil liberties organizations, worked with the NCAPT to get legislation passed to end the poll tax. They had some success on the state level, and by the 1960s only five states (Alabama, Arkansas, Mississippi, Texas, and Virginia) still had a poll tax.

More than 20 years after the creation of NCAPT, Congress finally proposed a poll tax constitutional amendment on August 17, 1962. The Twenty-fourth Amendment was ratified by the states on January 23, 1964. This amendment prohibited the paying of a poll tax as a requirement for voting in federal elections. It did not govern state and local elections. In the Deep South, state laws continued to deny the vote to African Americans, and civil rights workers increased their effort to gain African-American rights.

FREEDOM SUMMER

In 1964, three civil rights organizations—the Congress on Racial Equality (CORE), Student Nonviolent Coordinating Committee (SNCC), and the NAACP—organized the Freedom Summer campaign. A large number of civil rights workers participated in this campaign to end the disenfranchisement of African Americans in the South. They focused on Mississippi, a state with less than 7 percent of its large black population registered to vote. Workers representing all races came from other states to help in the voter registration drive.

Unfortunately, southern hatred and prejudice erupted into violence against the civil rights workers. Twenty black churches that served as a base for voter registration and education were firebombed and burned. James Chaney, Andrew Goodman, and Michael Schwerner, one black and two white civil rights workers who had been registering blacks to vote, arrived in Philadelphia, Mississippi, on June 21, 1964, to investigate the burning of Mt. Zion Church. That afternoon, the three men were arrested on a minor traffic violation and held for several hours. They were released but stopped again by Deputy Sheriff Cecil Price, who turned them over to Ku Klux Klan members. Their bodies were found about six weeks later on August 4, 1964. Violence continued throughout the summer. In December 1964, 19 men, including the deputy sheriff, were charged with civil rights violations but not murder. (In 1967, seven of the 19 were convicted on federal conspiracy charges and sent to prison. On January 7, 2005, Edgar Killen—one of the original 19 men—was charged with three counts of murder.)

MISSISSIPPI FREEDOM DEMOCRATIC PARTY

The effort to enfranchise (gain the vote for) blacks included an effort to gain entrance into the all-white Democratic Party in Mississippi. Fannie Lou Hamer (who did not know she had the right to vote until she attended a meeting of the Student Nonviolent Coordinating Committee [SNCC]) helped organize the Mississippi Freedom Democratic Party (MFDP). Eighty thousand black voters joined the MFDP. They elected 68 delegates to attend the 1964 Democratic National Convention in Atlantic City, New Jersey. Although the delegation was refused seating at the convention, its presence drew attention to 80,000 registered black Mississippi voters. Incumbent presidential candidate Lyndon B. Johnson and other congressional candidates from the South recognized the black voters' potential impact on future elections. Consequently, some of them wanted to win the support of these voters by addressing issues that were important to them.

Fannie Lou Hamer attended the National Democratic Convention in Atlantic City, New Jersey, in August 1964. *(Library of Congress, Prints and Photographs Division [LC-U9-12470b-17])*

VOTING RIGHTS ACT

Johnson won the 1964 election. After taking office in 1965, he began working with Congress to pass a voting rights bill. On August 6, 1965, President Johnson signed the Voting Rights Act of 1965 that temporarily suspended literacy tests and provided for the appointment of federal examiners with the power to register qualified citizens to vote.

The Voting Rights Act did not address the poll tax for state and local elections. Instead, it directed the U.S. attorney general to bring the matter before the U.S. Supreme Court. The Court ruled that the Virginia poll tax violated the equal protection of the law guaranteed in the Fourteenth Amendment. As Supreme Court deci-

After signing the Voting Rights Act in 1965, President Lyndon B. Johnson continued his effort to protect the rights of blacks by signing the Civil Rights Bill in 1968. *(Library of Congress, U.S. News & World Report Magazine Photograph Collection [LC-U9-18985-18A])*

sions may override other prior court decisions, this ruling made the poll tax unconstitutional in all states.

Four amendments to the U.S. Constitution and acts of Congress have clearly defined African Americans' civil rights, including the right to vote. Prejudice and hatred cannot be eliminated by legislation, and there are still people who violate and suppress the rights of others. Still, the African-American experience is an example of the importance of the right to vote and its power to protect freedom; those who do not have the vote are at the mercy of those who do.

3

Women Gain
the Right to Vote

Abigail Adams may have been the first woman to lobby Congress for women's rights. While her husband, John Adams, worked with the Congress to prepare the Declaration of Independence, Abigail wrote this warning to him on March 31, 1776,

> . . . in the new code of laws which I suppose it will be necessary for you to make, I desire you would remember the ladies . . . If particular care and attention is not paid to the ladies, we are determined to foment a Rebellion, and will not hold ourselves bound by the Laws in which we have no voice, or Representation.

Although Adams valued his wife's advice, the "ladies" were not remembered, and the power of the vote was placed into the hands of their husbands.

Who would have the vote was left to the states to decide, and all but one limited the vote to property-owning white men over age 21.

NEW JERSEY

The 1776 New Jersey constitution granted suffrage to "all inhabitants of this Colony, of full age, who are worth fifty pounds proclamation money . . . and have resided in the county in which they claim a vote for twelve months immediately preceding the election." Unfortunately, a married woman's property and money belonged to her husband. Consequently, only single women qualified to vote.

In the 1790s and early 1800s, large numbers of unmarried New Jersey women voted in elections and spoke out on political issues.

NO RIGHTS FOR WOMEN

American colonial laws were based on English common law, which made a married woman the property of her husband. Although a wife could not be bought and sold, her husband had complete control over her body, any property she owned before the marriage, and her wages if she worked outside the home.

Divorce placed the married woman in a horrifying situation. Marriage had stripped the wife of her property, so the divorced woman owned nothing. Furthermore, in the event of divorce, custody of the children remained with the father. Life was no easier for widows. In some states, the wife could not inherit her husband's property. Consequently, when a man with a family died, his widow was left with children to feed, clothe, and shelter, and no means to do so. Other women suffered hardships created by irresponsible husbands. These men drank and gambled away money needed to buy food and pay the rent. In addition, some wives were mentally and physically abused. As long as women did not have the right to vote, candidates and elected officials paid little attention to their problems. No laws were passed to improve their lives.

Single (never married) women had a few legal rights. They could own property and pay taxes but could not vote.

Restrictions on women began in childhood. Girls did not have the educational opportunities their brothers enjoyed. While boys were encouraged to study math and science, most girls were limited to reading, writing, music, dancing, needlework, and the proper way to pour tea for guests.

In 1807, however, New Jersey legislature passed an act limiting the vote to "free, white male citizens of the state, of the age of twenty-one years, worth fifty pounds proclamation money." This act disenfranchised women and free blacks in the state. After having the vote for more than 30 years, the leaders among these women had political experience, and they made use of the remaining tools available to them—the First Amendment rights to petition government and free speech.

WOMEN ACTIVISTS

Many women believed that all citizens should share in the pursuit of life, liberty, and happiness guaranteed in the U.S. Constitution. These women wanted to be able to cast a vote to help choose the leaders of America. They also wanted to have the opportunity to run for office and serve if elected. Many leaders of the suffrage (voting rights) movement were among the first women to receive a college

Many suffragists worked hard to gain the vote for women. Some began their work in the abolition movement. When women did not gain the vote along with black men, they began the struggle for women's rights. *(Library of Congress, Prints and Photographs Division [LC-USZ62-5535])*

degree in their chosen field. Some had the support of their families, while others had struggled on their own to gain an education. These women possessed talent and leadership qualities they wanted to use for the betterment of society. Although society did not allow women to speak in public at the time, even so, some of these women did. Most of them had strong opinions about slavery. This is where they began the struggle that would eventually gain their right to vote.

Angelina and Sarah Grimké

The Grimké sisters, daughters of a South Carolina slave-owning judge and planter, were the only southern white women to become abolition leaders. Angelina took her first stand against slavery in a letter to William Lloyd Garrison, the editor of an abolition newspaper, *The Liberator,* in 1835. The next year, Angelina published a pamphlet that encouraged southern women to join the antislavery cause. The American Anti-Slavery Society distributed Angelina Grimké's *Appeal to the Christian Women of the South* in the North. As a result of the popularity of her published views, Angelina was invited to speak at antislavery women's meetings.

Sarah Grimké soon joined her sister in antislavery activities. Angelina was a gifted speaker and Sarah was a talented writer. In 1837, the sisters began a lecture tour throughout New England. The tour launched the formation of many local women's antislavery societies and a massive petition campaign. The tour ended in 1838 with Angelina testifying before the Massachusetts legislature. (She was the first woman to speak before a legislative body in America.) As a part of her testimony, she presented antislavery petitions bearing tens of thousands of signatures. These signatures had been gathered in a huge petition drive that demonstrated the potential power of woman voters.

While women fought for the rights of slaves, some of them began to think of pursuing rights for themselves. The Grimké sisters began comparing the conditions of slaves with the conditions of women in their speeches and writings.

Expressing political views publicly was not an accepted activity for women in the 1830s. Consequently, the sisters were attacked in the press, from the pulpit, and by some male abolitionists. Threats of violence against the sisters made it difficult for them to find lecture halls where they could speak. In addition, the Massachusetts

"I am persuaded that the rights of woman, like the rights of slaves, need only be examined to be understood and asserted."

—*Sarah M. Grimké,* Letters on the Equality of the Sexes and the Condition of Woman, *1837*

General Association of Congregational Churches issued a pastoral letter stating that "women who took on such activist roles called their own chastity into question." In response to the pastoral letter, Sarah wrote letters addressing women's rights to Mary Parker, president of the Boston Female Anti-Slavery Society. *The Liberator,* an abolitionist newspaper in Boston, Massachusetts, published Sarah's 15 "Letters on the Equality of the Sexes and the Condition of Women" as a series. She wrote that "Men and women were CREATED EQUAL; they are both moral and accountable beings, and whatever is *right* for man to do, is *right* for woman." The Grimké sisters were the first link between abolitionists and the future women's suffrage movement. About 10 years after Sarah Grimké wrote her equality letters, two new leaders emerged from the anti-slavery movement to take the first step toward empowering women with the right to vote.

SENECA FALLS

The women's suffrage movement formally began in July 1848 at Seneca Falls, New York. The idea was born at a social gathering attended by Elizabeth Cady Stanton, Lucretia Mott, Martha C. Wright (Mott's sister), Mary Ann McClintock, and Jane Hunt. That afternoon, these women determined that the time had come for the oppression of women to be laid before the public. They decided that they would begin the task at a small convention.

Elizabeth Cady Stanton wrote the Declaration of Sentiments that was presented at the convention. Using the Declaration of Independence as a guide, she declared that "all Men and women are created equal, that they are endowed by their Creator with certain unalienable Rights." She also included a list of 18 "repeated injuries and usurpations on the part of man toward woman, having in direct object the establishment of an absolute tyranny over her."

Stanton and Mott were the major organizers of the Seneca Falls Convention, and they advertised it in the local newspaper, the *Seneca County Courier.* The convention took place on July 19–20, 1848, at the Wesleyan Chapel.

A committee of women met to discuss and amend the Declaration of Sentiments along with 11 resolutions on Wednesday morning, July 19, 1848. The ninth resolution stated that "it is the duty

"The right [to vote] is ours. Have it, we must. Use it, we will. The pens, the tongues, the fortunes, the indomitable wills of many women are already pledged to secure this right."

—*Elizabeth Cady Stanton speaking at the first women's rights convention in Seneca Falls, New York, July 20, 1848*

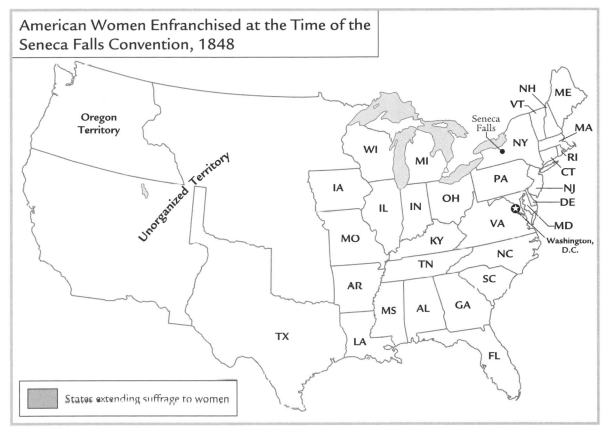

American Women Enfranchised at the Time of the Seneca Falls Convention, 1848

States extending suffrage to women

As shown on this map, no states allowed women to vote in 1848.

of the women of this country to secure to themselves their sacred right to the elective franchise."

The idea of securing voting rights for women shocked some of the committee members. Elizabeth Cady Stanton later recalled Lucretia Mott's response, "Why, Lizzie, thee will make us ridiculous." Stanton stood firm on the ninth resolution.

The next day, the Declaration of Sentiments was presented to the whole convention, about 300 people (including men). Most of the attendees were Quakers, a Christian denomination that allowed women more freedom to speak than did other denominations. Many of the people who attended were also activists in the antislavery movement. By the end of the day, 100 people had signed the Declaration of Sentiments—68 women and 32 men. Later, when controversies arose, many of them removed their names. Still, as the organizers had intended, it was a beginning. Other activists soon realized that women's suffrage was the way to accomplish their goals, such as restricting the sale of alcohol (temperance).

SUSAN B. ANTHONY

Susan B. Anthony was actively involved in the temperance movement when she met Elizabeth Cady Stanton in 1851. A friendship developed between the two activists, and they began supporting each other's cause. In 1853, Anthony was denied the right to speak at a state convention of the Sons of Temperance because she was a woman. After this experience, Anthony recognized that women needed the vote to be effective political activists. She then focused her attention on gaining the vote for women. She later stated that "the right which woman needed above every other, the one indeed which would secure to her all the others, was the right of suffrage."

THE BATTLE INTENSIFIES

In about 1868, Susan B. Anthony and Elizabeth Cady Stanton formed the American Equal Rights Association. To give the association a voice, they began publishing a suffrage newspaper, *The Revolution.* The masthead included their slogan "Men, their rights, and nothing more; women, their rights and nothing less." The goal of the newspaper was to promote "justice for all."

In 1869, the suffrage movement split into two organizations. The National Woman Suffrage Association (NWSA), founded by Anthony and Stanton, focused attention on gaining women's suffrage nationwide by adding a suffrage amendment to the U.S. Constitution. The American Woman Suffrage Association (AWSA), founded by Lucy Stone, Henry Blackwell, and Julia Ward Howe, worked to gain the vote for women through state legislation, state by state.

THE OPPOSITION

As the suffrage movement gained strength, organizations formed to oppose the vote for women. Some businesses and industries supported antisuffrage organizations. For example, liquor industry leaders knew that many women wanted stronger laws to control alcohol sales. They thought that women would vote candidates into office who would pass legislation that would decrease their profits.

Other businesses that needed large labor forces also supported antisuffrage organizations. At this time, wages were low, and there were no requirements for companies to provide safe working conditions or limit working hours. Many owners and managers of businesses knew that many women were concerned about child labor practices, unequal pay, low wages, and poor working conditions. They thought that women with the vote would elect legislators who would pass labor laws.

Antisuffrage activists promoted the idea that women belonged in the home. They argued that women with the vote would damage the American home and children. They questioned women's ability to cast an intelligent vote. In addition, they spread the word that most women did not want the vote. They made speeches and published broadsides (one-page newspapers) and fliers ridiculing suffragists in cartoons and essays.

Some of these people knew that women should have the vote. Still, they did not want them to have it.

> "I think I could write a pretty strong argument in favor of female suffrage, but I do not want to do it. I never want to see women voting, and gabbling about politics, and electioneering. There is something revolting in the thought. It would shock me inexpressibly for an angel to come down from above and ask me to take a drink with him (though I should doubtless consent); but it would shock me still more to see one of our blessed earthly angels peddling election tickets among a mob of shabby scoundrels she never saw before."
>
> —Mark Twain, The Democrat, *St. Louis, Missouri, March 15, 1867*

CASTING ILLEGAL BALLOTS

Suffragists insisted that, as U.S. citizens, women had a constitutional right to vote. They wanted to test this belief in the courts. Their plan was for women to attempt to register and vote. When one of them was denied this right, legal action would be brought against the officials who denied a woman the right to vote. They believed they could win the right to vote in court.

From 1868 to 1873, hundreds of women tried to register and vote. A few successfully cast ballots in local elections. These illegal ballots were quietly tossed out without being counted. Until late 1872, most election officials extended tolerance to the women who attempted to vote and did not charge them with illegal voting.

Arrested!

On November 5, 1872, Susan B. Anthony successfully cast a ballot in a federal election. She wrote to Elizabeth Cady Stanton that day:

Women had the right to vote in many states before passage of the Nineteenth Amendment granted women suffrage in all states. This photo shows New York women voting for the first time. *(Library of Congress, Prints and Photographs Division [LC-USZ62-75334])*

"Well, I have been & gone & done it!!—positively voted the Republican ticket—straight this a.m. at 7 O'clock." Much to her surprise, on November 18, Susan B. Anthony was arrested for illegal voting and held for $1,000 bail. On January 1, 1873, she wrote, "I never dreamed of the U.S. officers prosecuting me for voting—thought only that if I was refused—I should bring action against inspectors." Still, the hope was that the case could be used to get a U.S. Supreme Court ruling on women's suffrage. The judge, however, prevented Anthony's case from going to the jury. He fined her $100 plus court costs. Anthony refused to pay, and the judge responded, "Madam, the Court will not order you committed until the fine is paid." Anthony did not pay and the judge did not sentence her to jail. The episode ended in a standoff that could not be appealed to a higher court.

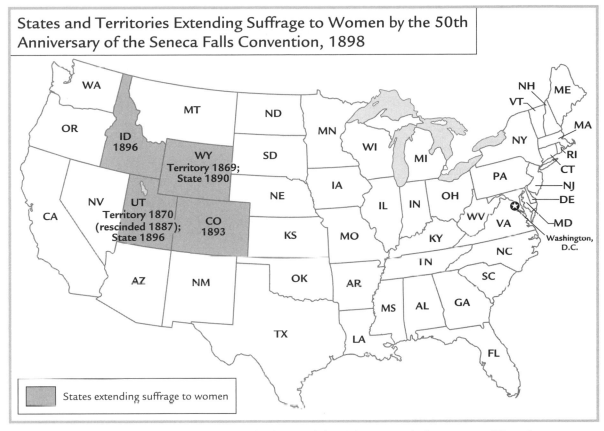

States and Territories Extending Suffrage to Women by the 50th Anniversary of the Seneca Falls Convention, 1898

States extending suffrage to women

By 1898, after 50 years of hard work, women had gained the right to vote in four states—Wyoming, Colorado, Utah, and Idaho.

Failing to bring women's suffrage to the courts, Susan B. Anthony made a new plan of attack. She began a campaign to circulate petitions for a women's suffrage amendment to the Constitution. By 1877, women had gathered 10,000 signatures from people in 26 states. Anthony presented the petition to Congress in 1878 and continued to bring the request for a suffrage amendment before Congress every year thereafter. When she became too frail, others continued her work. The proposed amendment was presented to Congress each year from 1878 to 1919, when if finally passed.

THE NEXT GENERATION

The next generation of women's suffrage leaders included Carrie Chapman Catt, Alice Paul, Lucy Burns, and Harriot Stanton Blatch

(Elizabeth Cady Stanton's daughter). As these women rose to leadership positions in the American suffrage movement, they began to use more aggressive methods similar to those being used by suffragists in England. These included large parades and picketing.

The first major suffrage parade was held in New York City in 1910. The Woman's Political Union under the leadership of Harriot Stanton Blanch organized the parade. A larger parade in New York City in 1912 included 20,000 women and 500 men marchers with 500,000 onlookers lining the parade route. Parades were held in other major cities, some more spectacular than others. Inez Milholland Boissevain became famous for leading parades riding a white horse and dressed in an elaborate costume including a flowing white cape.

On March 3, 1913 (the eve of President Woodrow Wilson's inauguration), the National American Woman Suffrage Association (NAWSA) staged a spectacular event in Washington, D.C. Inez Milholland Boissevain led the parade, followed by marchers, floats, and banners. A grand finale was performed on the steps of the Treasury Building.

A large crowd (mostly men who had come to Washington to attend Wilson's inauguration) lined the street. After the procession had advanced a few blocks, the crowd surged into the street blocking the parade route. The New York *Evening Journal* reported the next day that "Women were jeered, tripped, grabbed, shoved, and

EYEWITNESS ACCOUNT OF THE 1913 WASHINGTON, D.C., SUFFRAGE PARADE

The pageant began with "The Star Spangled Banner" and the commanding figure of Columbia dressed in national colors, emerging from the great columns at the top of the Treasury Building steps. Charity entered, her path strewn with rose petals; Liberty followed to the "Triumphal March" from Aida, and a dove of peace was released. In the final tableau [scene], Columbia, surrounded by Justice, Charity, Liberty, Peace and Hope, all in flowing robes and colorful scarves, with trumpets sounding, stood to watch the oncoming procession.

—Sheridan Harvey, New York *Evening Journal*, March 4, 1913

many heard 'indecent epithets' and 'barnyard conversation.'" Although about 100 marchers were injured and taken to the hospital by ambulance, others reached the Treasury Building. The parade ended with a breathtaking production number promoting equality and woman suffrage.

By 1915, women had won full suffrage in 11 states, including Wyoming, Colorado, Utah, Washington, California, Oregon, Arizona, Kansas, Nevada, Idaho, and Montana. Women in these states showed that they were a power to be considered in the political scene. Within a year after granting woman suffrage in 1914, Montana sent Jeannette Rankin to Washington as its representative in the U.S. Congress.

WORLD WAR I

The United States entered World War I in 1917. For the duration of the war, women's suffrage activity declined while many women responded to the national crisis. They filled job vacancies left when American men went to war and took their place in the workforce needed to produce supplies for the troops.

Some women did continue the suffrage effort. Alice Paul and her followers formed the National Women's Party. They began picketing the White House in an effort to gain President Wilson's support for women's suffrage. As they continued the picket line through the war years, their picket signs accused Wilson of being a hypocrite. They asked why he sent American men to die in a war for democracy in Europe while denying American women the right to vote. Their waved signs that asked, "Mr. President, how long must women wait for liberty?"

While America was at war, many people were offended by this attack on the president. Some bystanders made verbal attacks on the picketers. When this escalated to physical attacks, the police did nothing to protect the women. Instead, they began arresting the picketers. Most of the suffragists were jailed for only a few days. Alice Paul, however, was sentenced to seven months in prison. She responded by going on a hunger strike. Afraid she might die, prison doctors force-fed Paul three times a day for three weeks. Newspapers covered her ordeal in detail. Their reports drew sympathy for Paul and for women's suffrage. After five weeks, Paul was released from prison.

While Paul became a media attraction, other women gained recognition for their role in managing the home front while American men were at war in Europe. This elevated the view of woman's citizenship to one of greater respect and made women's suffrage acceptable to more people. In 1919, the number of states granting full suffrage to women reached 15 with the addition of New York, Michigan, Oklahoma, and South Dakota.

NINETEENTH AMENDMENT

A breakthrough on the national level came on January 9, 1918, when President Wilson announced his support for women's suffrage. The next day, the U.S. House of Representatives passed the Susan B. Anthony Amendment. The amendment passed in the Senate by one vote on June 4, 1919. Two years and nine months after its passage in the House, Tennessee became the 36th state to ratify the Nineteenth Amendment to the U.S. Constitution. On

Kentucky governor Edwin P. Morrow signed the Nineteenth Amendment on January 6, 1920, making Kentucky the 24th state to ratify the amendment. Twelve more states were needed to add the Nineteenth Amendment to the Constitution and grant women the right to vote in the United States. *(Library of Congress, Prints and Photographs Division [LC-USZ62-78691])*

August 16, 1920, after a 72-year struggle, U.S. women had the right to vote. Eight million women went to the polls in the 1920 presidential election. Only one woman who attended the conference at Seneca Falls, however, lived to see women gain the right to vote. By this time, Charlotte Woodward was 102 years old and too frail to cast her vote in the 1920 election.

With their mission finally accomplished, women's suffrage activists took on a new role. They formed the League of Women Voters in 1920, with Carrie Chapman Catt serving as the first president. The new organization worked to educate American women in the use of their vote and to draw them together in support of certain issues. This organization is still a respected force in American politics.

4

Others Gain the Vote

With the ratification of the Nineteenth Amendment in 1920, all mentally able U.S. citizens over age 21 not in prison convicted of a felony had a constitutional right to register and vote in the state where they lived. Still, this left many people living in the United States without the vote, including some American Indians and immigrants.

NATURALIZED CITIZENS

The first voters added to the U.S. electorate were qualifying naturalized citizens—legal immigrants who earned U.S. citizenship. Congress passed the first Naturalization Act in 1790. This act set federal rules to be used in all states for the naturalization process. It required that immigrants live in the United States for two years before they could acquire citizenship. Since then, several congressional acts have changed the naturalization requirements, extending the residency requirement to five years and limiting travel outside the United States during this time. Basically, a legal immigrant must live in the United States for the required period of time to establish residency with the intent to make his or her home in the United States. In addition, the immigrant must learn some U.S. history, how the government works (civics), and basic English. After passing a test, the immigrant must pledge allegiance to the United States and agree to uphold the Constitution and laws of the land.

Naturalization ceremonies are held several times a year in major cities across the nation. Senator Lamar Alexander (Republican–Tennessee) described a naturalization ceremony he witnessed on

Eastern European immigrants huddle on the deck of the SS *Amsterdam* on their way to America in 1899. Many immigrants found jobs in American industry. Within a few years of arrival, they had the opportunity to become naturalized U.S. citizens with the right to vote. *(Library of Congress, Prints and Photographs Division [LC-USZ62-95431])*

September 17, 2003: "There were 77 persons from 22 countries who had passed their exams, learned English, passed a test about American government, survived a character investigation, paid their taxes, and waited in line for five years to be a citizen of the United States of America." At the completion of each ceremony, the new citizens swear an oath of allegiance to the United States. Once an immigrant has taken the oath of naturalization, he or she becomes a U.S. citizen with the right to vote.

Many immigrants follow family members to the United States. Sometimes family members sponsor the immigrant relative by

OATH OF ALLEGIANCE

Dating back to 1790, the oath was adopted as a federal regulation in 1929 and assumed its present form in the 1950s. The oath is solemnly repeated by every candidate for citizenship during the naturalization ceremony.

> *I hereby declare, on oath, that I absolutely and entirely renounce and abjure all allegiance and fidelity to any foreign prince, potentate, state or sovereignty, of whom or which I have heretofore been a subject or citizen; that I will support and defend the Constitution and laws of the United States of America against all enemies, foreign and domestic; that I will bear true faith and allegiance to the same; that I will bear arms on behalf of the United States when required by the law; that I will perform noncombatant service in the armed forces of the United States when required by the law; that I will perform work of national importance under civilian direction when required by the law; and that I take this obligation freely without any mental reservation or purpose of evasion; so help me God.*

agreeing to house and support them until they find a job. Consequently, naturalized citizens often join relatives in an ethnic community where they share a similar culture and common interests. Ethnic groups have political issues that are important to them, and candidates running for office often seek their votes by supporting these issues. For example, farm labor conditions in U.S.-Mexican border states, bilingual education, and the treatment of undocumented immigrants are important issues to Mexican-American voters. Most members of ethnic minority groups are interested in voting for candidates who understand their culture and share their concerns. They want to use their vote to elect candidates who will help pass legislation that will protect their civil rights, fight racism and prejudice, and respect their culture and ancestry while improving education and career opportunities. Elected officials who want to stay in office listen to the people who voted for them and consider their views when debating new legislation. This is the power of the vote.

The Naturalization Acts gave people who moved to the United States from other nations a way to become U.S. citizens with a voice in government. American Indians, although considered citizens of a tribal nation, could not gain citizenship through naturalization.

This 1867 political cartoon mocks California Republican gubernatorial nominee George C. Gorhman's belief that voting rights should be given to all minority men. Even this radical Californian was not accused of considering voting rights for women. *(Library of Congress, Prints and Photographs Division [LC-USZ62-702])*

AMERICAN INDIANS

American Indians, who are now an ethnic minority in U.S. society, were once the majority population on the North American continent. For this reason, when European nations established colonies along the Atlantic coast of North America, they dealt with the Indians by negotiating treaties. When the colonies became the United States, the practice continued. The American Indians considered themselves citizens of sovereign nations (their tribes) with their own governing leaders. They did not seek U.S. citizenship. In the 19th century, while blacks and women fought long battles for citizenship and the vote, American Indians fought to regain homelands, preserve tribal identity, their cultures, and their old way of life.

The way of life for many tribes required that the heartland of America remain an open wilderness for hunting, fishing, and foraging. This conflicted with the American dream of owning land, farming, ranching, mining the natural resources, and building towns and cities. The U.S. government wanted to convert the Indians to this way of life. They thought that U.S. citizenship would help to bring the Indians into mainstream America. Therefore, they looked for opportunities to grant Indians citizenship in exchange for assimilation into mainstream society. For example, when groups of American Indians were forced westward by treaty, Indians were given the opportunity to own land as individuals (as opposed to their traditional tribal ownership) and become U.S. citizens. Indians who chose to live a "civilized" life or adopted the Christian religion could also become citizens. In 1888, Congress granted citizenship to American Indian wives of U.S. citizens.

Gaining U.S. citizenship, however, required giving up tribal membership and swearing loyalty to the United States (similar to becoming a naturalized citizen). It would, therefore, also mean giving up the struggle for rights and lands that had been taken from their tribe. Most Indians did not want to separate from their tribe or give up the struggle for their land, and they refused U.S. citizenship. They moved with the tribe to smaller areas "reserved" for them (reservations) in exchange for ceding original homelands. Reservation Indians retained their tribal identity but lost much of their culture. The treaties and relocation, moreover, did not convert the hunters to farmers. Often the new land they were assigned was very poor and unsuitable for farming.

By treaty, a nation-to-nation relationship existed between the United States and each Indian nation. When tribal leaders went to Washington, they were treated as officials from small foreign nations with little power. The Indian people had no rights as U.S. citizens, and without the power of the vote, they had no representation in U.S. Congress. Therefore, when Congress dealt with Indian nations, they favored the best interest of U.S. citizens—who demanded opening reservation lands for white settlement.

In 1887, Congress passed the Dawes Act, named for its author, Senator Henry Dawes of Massachusetts. This act gave the president of the United States the authority to divide the Indian reservations among individuals. The small parcels of land (usually 160 acres) given each qualified tribe member were called allotments. This act was intended to force Indians to accept a more mainstream way of life. Henry Dawes believed that once Indians owned property they would "wear civilized clothes . . . cultivate the ground, live in houses, ride in Studebaker wagons, [and] send children to school . . ." Indians who accepted an allotment were offered U.S.

THE DAWES ACT

The Dawes Act moved Indians from the tribal, shared reservations to individual parcels of land. Indians who did not have the right to vote had no voice in this decision.

And every Indian born within the territorial limits of the United States to whom allotments shall have been made under the provisions of this act, or under any law or treaty, and every Indian born within the territorial limits of the United States who has voluntarily taken up, within said limits, his residence separate and apart from any tribe of Indians therein, and has adopted the habits of civilized life, is hereby declared to be a citizen of the United States, and is entitled to all the rights, privileges, and immunities of such citizens, whether said Indian has been or not, by birth or otherwise, a member of any tribe of Indians within the territorial limits of the United States without in any manner affecting the right of any such Indian to tribal or other property.

—The Dawes Act, 1887

citizenship. Male Indian citizens who owned land and paid taxes could vote.

According to the Dawes Act, after all qualified Indians had received an allotment, the remaining land could be divided into 160-acre homesteads and opened for white settlement. This led to the loss of huge amounts of tribal land.

Indians could claim their allotment by meeting the qualifications of tribal membership and adding their name to the tribal roll. The federal government (and most tribes) requires one-quarter "quantum blood" Indian to receive federal Indian benefits or tribe membership. Quantum blood is the amount of Indian or tribal blood a person inherits from parents. For example, if a full-blood Comanche marries a non-Comanche, the children of that union will be one-half quantum blood Comanche. The quantum blood is reduced by half as it passes from parent to child. The amount passed to the child from each parent is added together—a child who received one-eighth from one parent and one-eighth from the other would be one-quarter quantum blood and qualify for tribal membership.

Some tribes successfully delayed the breakup of their reservation when members refused to place their name on the tribal roll. Others, such as the Five Civilized Tribes—as the Cherokee, Chickasaw, Creek, Choctaw, and Seminole were then known—were not reservation tribes and were not included in the Dawes Act. They had been forced from much of their original homeland in the East in the 19th century. They had been given lands in Indian Territory (Oklahoma). They managed to hold their land in Indian Territory until Oklahoma became a state in 1907. At that time, the Chickasaw, Choctaw, Cherokee, Seminole, and Creek began to lose their land. The last tribal land was allotted on June 14, 1914 (27 years after the passage of the Dawes Act). As these Indians acquired allotments, they were eligible for U.S. citizenship.

After World War I, Congress offered citizenship to about 9,000 Indians who had served in the U.S. military. By 1920, through various treaties and congressional acts, about two-thirds of the American Indian population was eligible for citizenship.

In 1924, President Calvin Coolidge signed a bill granting all Indians born in the territorial United States full citizenship. The 1924 American Indian Citizenship Act allowed Indians to keep

AMERICAN INDIAN CITIZENSHIP ACT

Be it enacted . . . that every American Indian who served in the Military or Naval Establishments of the United States during the war against the Imperial German Government, and who has received or who shall hereafter receive an honorable discharge, if not now a citizen and if he so desires, shall, on proof of such discharge and after proper identification before a court of competent jurisdiction, and without other examination except as prescribed by said court, be granted full citizenship with all the privileges pertaining thereto, without in any manner impairing or otherwise affecting the property rights, individuals or tribal, of any such Indian or his interest in tribal or other Indian property.

—American Indian Citizenship Act, November 6, 1919

their tribal citizenship along with U.S. citizenship. Still, some state laws denied Indians the right to vote for many years. Arizona withheld the vote from American Indians until 1948. Indians received the right to vote in Utah in 1953, Maine in 1954, and New Mexico in 1962. Today, American Indians qualify to vote in all elections—tribal, local, state, and federal. They have dual citizenship.

For more than six decades after the first Indians gained suffrage, most tribes discouraged voting. "It was taboo. Why would you want to mess around in a non-Indian election when we were supposed to be sovereign?" explained Kurt Luger, head of the Great Plains Indian Gaming Association. In addition, many Indians did not trust white politicians. Furthermore, American Indians represent a very small portion of the U.S. population. They did not think their small number of votes made a difference.

This attitude began to change in 1988, when Congress approved the Indian Gaming Regulatory Act. Gambling became legal on Indian lands and tribes began opening casinos. Indian land is located within states. Consequently, Congress gave the states some limited authority over Indian gambling. Operating the casinos gave the Indians a greater interest in local and national elections, and the gambling revenue increased the political clout of this small minority. They had large tribal funds and could invest in the campaigns of candidates who supported their political interests.

"These are people [American Indians] who have been pushed around, and when they haven't been pushed around, they have been ignored. Both political parties are going to have to start listening to them with some respect."

—*Senator Tim Johnson (Democrat–South Dakota), October 2, 2003*

In the 2000 presidential election, the national electorate was divided almost equally between Republicans and Democrats. In some states, the Indian vote could have changed the outcome of the election. Today, Indians are more interested in politics and have organized efforts to "get out the Indian vote."

American Indian voters share many concerns with other U.S. voters such as jobs, health care, foreign policy. In addition, they are often concerned about issues relating to their culture, burial grounds and holy places, native religion, lands, commercial interests, protecting the environment, and preserving their languages. American Indian voters also want to elect candidates who understand tribal law and the effect of U.S. government policies toward the tribes.

TEEN VOTERS

In the 1960s, many young people became political activists. Some Native American young people held protests for Indian rights. Other young people worked for civil rights for women and blacks. Still others protested against the Vietnam War. Flower children, hippies, protesters, and peace marchers introduced America to the political energies of youth. Some of these protesters called attention to the fact that 18-year-olds were being sent to war in Vietnam and being killed. Eighteen was old enough to serve in the U.S. military. Eighteen was not old enough to vote in elections that would decide who would send America's young men into battle. Activists began lobbying Congress to lower the voting age to 18. They wanted people who could be drafted to serve in the military to have the right to vote.

In 1970, Congress passed legislation that extended the Voting Rights Act of 1965 and attached an amendment that lowered the voting age to 18 in state, local, and federal elections. Some states believed that the act interfered with the states' power to control their own elections, a power reserved for them in the U.S. Constitution. The 1970 Voting Rights Act was challenged by several states and reached the U.S. Supreme Court as *Oregon v. Mitchell* (Mitchell was the U.S. attorney general). The U.S. Supreme Court ruled that Congress has the authority to permit 18-year-old citizens to vote in national elections but does not have the power to change state and local election laws. To make the minimum voting age uniform in all elections, Congress presented the Twenty-sixth Amendment to the states for ratification in 1971. Most states agreed that 18-year-olds should have the right to vote. The Twenty-sixth Amendment was ratified by the legislatures of the required 38 states in little more than two months— record time for ratification of a constitutional amendment.

Approximately 58 percent of more than 11 million young Americans age 18 to 20 registered to vote for the first time in the 1972 presidential election. About 48 percent (more than 5 million) voted that November. President Richard M. Nixon won the electoral votes of 49 states for one of the biggest landslide victories in American history. First-time voters who supported Nixon's Democratic challenger George McGovern may have suffered disappointment in the overwhelming loss. In the following

Eighteen and eligible to vote for the first time, Shannon Marie studies a sample ballot, preparing for the next election. *(Photo by author)*

presidential elections, voter registration and number of votes cast in this age range continually dropped. Census Bureau statistics for the 2000 election showed voter registration for this age group at 40 percent and the votes cast at little more than 28 percent. This represents an 18-point drop in registration and a 20-point drop in votes cast.

Many young people say the reason they do not vote is that they lack information about the issues and candidates. They do not get the information they need because most candidates focus their campaigns on older citizens, who are more likely to vote.

Several nonpartisan organizations are trying to increase the number of young voters. For example, Youth Vote 2000 worked to encourage young voters in the 2000 election. A similar group formed for the 2002 election. Another nonpartisan organization, Campaign for Young Voters, develops material to help candidates reach young voters. This organization prepares material and compiles information for candidates throughout the nation for each election year. Hip-hop impresario Sean "P. Diddy" Combs's Citizen Change campaign challenged young voters to "Vote or Die," and

"Young people aren't voting because politicians aren't talking to them about the issues they care about. And politicians aren't talking to them about the issues they care about because young people don't vote."

—*Julia Cohen, executive director of Youth Vote 2000, a nonpartisan coalition dedicated to encouraging civic participation among American young people*

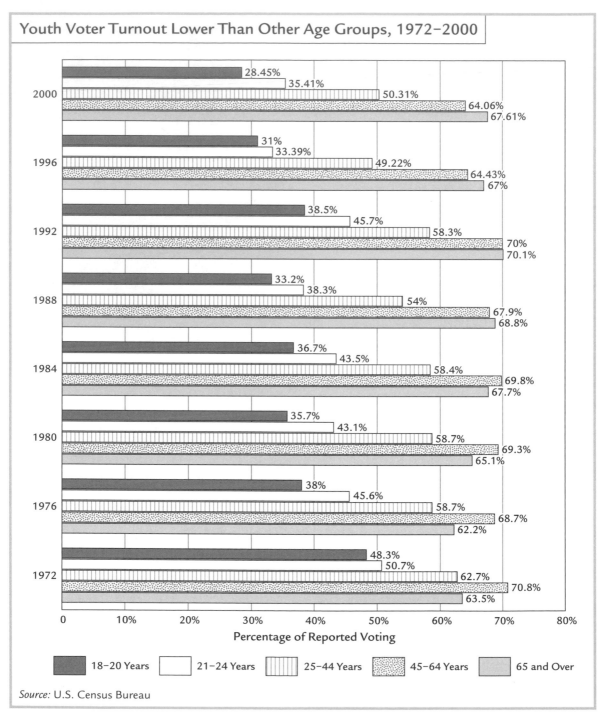

Youth Voter Turnout Lower Than Other Age Groups, 1972–2000

2000
- 18–20 Years: 28.45%
- 21–24 Years: 35.41%
- 25–44 Years: 50.31%
- 45–64 Years: 64.06%
- 65 and Over: 67.61%

1996
- 18–20 Years: 31%
- 21–24 Years: 33.39%
- 25–44 Years: 49.22%
- 45–64 Years: 64.43%
- 65 and Over: 67%

1992
- 18–20 Years: 38.5%
- 21–24 Years: 45.7%
- 25–44 Years: 58.3%
- 45–64 Years: 70%
- 65 and Over: 70.1%

1988
- 18–20 Years: 33.2%
- 21–24 Years: 38.3%
- 25–44 Years: 54%
- 45–64 Years: 67.9%
- 65 and Over: 68.8%

1984
- 18–20 Years: 36.7%
- 21–24 Years: 43.5%
- 25–44 Years: 58.4%
- 45–64 Years: 69.8%
- 65 and Over: 67.7%

1980
- 18–20 Years: 35.7%
- 21–24 Years: 43.1%
- 25–44 Years: 58.7%
- 45–64 Years: 69.3%
- 65 and Over: 65.1%

1976
- 18–20 Years: 38%
- 21–24 Years: 45.6%
- 25–44 Years: 58.7%
- 45–64 Years: 68.7%
- 65 and Over: 62.2%

1972
- 18–20 Years: 48.3%
- 21–24 Years: 50.7%
- 25–44 Years: 62.7%
- 45–64 Years: 70.8%
- 65 and Over: 63.5%

Percentage of Reported Voting

Legend: 18–20 Years | 21–24 Years | 25–44 Years | 45–64 Years | 65 and Over

Source: U.S. Census Bureau

Since the voting age was lowered to 18, the youth age-group has consistently had a lower voter turnout than other age groups.

Rock the Vote registered more than 1.4 million young voters in 2004.

Based on state and national exit polls, the Center for Information and Research on Civil Learning and Engagement (CIRCLE) estimates that 42 percent to 47 percent of eligible 18–24-year-olds voted in the 2004 presidential election. These figures show a youth voter turnout increase over the 2000 and 1996 presidential elections; however, they fall short of the 48 percent to 50 percent turnout for this age group in the 1992 presidential election. Voters in all age groups turned out in record numbers in 2004. As a result, the percent of 18–24-year-old voters in the total turnout remained about the same as 2000.

Young voters are affected by the same issues as other voters. The issues that most concern voters under age 20 are related to their location, ethnic background, and their parents' political views. Issues that top the concerns of voters of all ages in 2003 included terrorism, job availability, the economy, and crime. Issues in 2004 included national security, terrorism, the war in Iraq, moral values, job opportunities, and the economy. Many issues interest some age groups more than they interest others. For example, retired citizens are concerned about Medicare, prescription drug coverage, and Social Security. Many working people are concerned about government spending and payroll taxes. Issues that affect younger voters include government loans for college tuition, the economy, entry-level job opportunities, minimum wage, and job benefits such as health and dental insurance. All these issues, however, affect all citizens—the citizens who receive the benefits and the taxpayers who pay for them.

Successful candidates at the state and federal levels are the people who decide where tax dollars are spent, who will benefit most, and how much of a person's income will go for taxes. Knowing where candidates stand on the issues helps voters determine who will run the government more nearly to their liking. Unfortunately, young people with most of their tax-paying careers ahead of them and the most at stake are the least likely to vote.

Most people believe that all citizens should have the right to vote, except criminals serving time in prison and people who do not have the mental ability to make their own decisions. About half the people who believe citizens should have the right to vote deny themselves this right. They do not register, and they do not vote.

5

Primary and General Elections

THE PEOPLE'S POWER

Qualified citizens who choose to be voters take charge of the government through the election process. In fact, voters are the most powerful people in the United States. They determine who will hold the offices of authority in U.S. towns, cities, counties, and states as well as the highest offices in the federal government.

State and local elections are conducted according to each state's constitution and laws. These elections include candidates for school board members, city mayors, county officials, state legislators, and governors. The results of these elections are usually of little concern beyond city or county limits and state boundaries. Some state governorships, however, are of national interest because governors sometimes become presidential candidates. For example, James Earl Carter (Georgia), Ronald Reagan (California), William Jefferson Clinton (Arkansas), and George Walker Bush (Texas) were governors before they were elected president. Although sometimes of national concern, gubernatorial (of a governor) elections are conducted according to state constitutional guidelines.

Elections of state representatives to the federal government are held in the states as stipulated by the U.S. Constitution and are regulated by federal law. These include the election of members of the U.S. House of Representatives and the U.S. Senate as well as each state's electors, who will participate in electing the president and vice president. Today, each party's presidential candidate chooses a

> "The most important political office is that of the private citizen."
>
> —Louis Brandeis,
> Supreme Court justice,
> 1916–39

53

Every segment of adult American society has sought the power to vote. In this 1915 photo, suffragists express their desire for this power by carrying ballot boxes in a parade in New York City. *(Library of Congress, George Grantham Bain Collection [LC-USZ62-132968])*

vice presidential running mate at the party's national convention. They are placed on the November ballot together as a team.

CHOOSING PRESIDENTIAL CANDIDATES

The founding fathers did not include in the Constitution a method for choosing presidential candidates. From 1796 to 1824, Congress (a changing mix of Federalists, Democratic-Republicans, National Republicans, Coalition, and Jackson Democrats) nominated candidates for this high office. In accordance with the Constitution, after Congress nominated the presidential candidates, each state chose electors who cast the state's electoral votes. (The state legislatures selected the electors in most states.) There was no candidate nominated for vice president in the first four elections. The candidate who received the most votes became president. The candidate with the second-highest number became the vice president. In the 1800 election, however, Democratic-Republican nominees Thomas Jeffer-

CONSTITUTIONAL GUIDELINES FOR ELECTING THE U.S. PRESIDENT AND VICE PRESIDENT

The founding fathers included specific requirements for the election of the president and vice president. The 1800 election resulted in a tie between Thomas Jefferson and Aaron Burr. Consequently, the election was decided in the House of Representatives. As a result of this crisis, Congress proposed an amendment that required separate ballots listing the candidates for president and vice president. The Twelfth Amendment was ratified in 1804. Another problem surfaced in the 1836 election, when none of the four vice presidential candidates won a majority of the electoral vote and the vice president was elected in the Senate. The next year, William Henry Harrison and John Tyler ran as a president/vice president team with the campaign slogan "Tippecanoe and Tyler, too" and won the election. This practice continues today with the presidential nominee choosing a running mate to run on a president/vice president party ticket.

son and Aaron Burr (the party's choice for president and vice president, respectively) received the same number of votes. As a result of the tie vote for president, the election was decided in the House of Representatives. To prevent this from happening again, Congress proposed the Twelfth Amendment, which determined that the president and vice president would be elected on separate ballots.

In the early 1800s, political parties began nominating candidates for president. At about this time, states gradually began shifting the responsibility for choosing the state's electors to a vote of the people. The popular vote was recorded for the first time in 1824. In that election, no candidate among the three won a majority of the electoral vote. In fact, Andrew Jackson (Democratic-Republican) received more electoral votes than John Quincy Adams (Coalition) and won the popular vote. Still, in accordance with the U.S. Constitution, the election was decided in the House of Representatives. The representatives of each state cast one vote for one of the three presidential candidates who received the most electoral votes. With 25 states represented in the House, John Quincy Adams received a majority with 13 votes. Jackson received seven, and three votes went to the third candidate, William H. Crawford. With the exception of the 1800 and 1824 elections, U.S. presidents have been elected by the electors (the Electoral College) selected in the November general election.

The Presidential Primary

According to the Federal Election Commission (FEC),

> *Establishing the Date for a Presidential primary, and determining the type of Presidential primary held, varies from state to state. This is due to differences in state statutes, party constitutions, party rules and regulations, party by-laws, and delegate selection plans. In some states, a caucus and/or convention may be held instead of a Presidential primary election. Other states may use a combination of both caucuses and primaries for delegate selection.*

To become a major party's nominee, presidential candidates must win the support of a majority of the delegates to the party's national convention. Consequently, candidates for nomination tend to campaign in states where they have a chance to win and ignore the others. As a result, the number of candidates offered on the primary ballot varies from state to state.

These primary elections are conducted by state political party committees. Although each candidate's name appears on the ballot, voters are actually selecting the delegates to the party's national convention, who will cast the state's votes to nominate the party's presidential candidate. Some states have open primaries, in which each voter chooses a party ballot at the polls and votes for that party's candidates. Alaska, however, offers a blanket ballot to every voter. This ballot includes all candidates from all parties, so Alaska voters can vote for any party's candidate. Most states hold closed primaries. This means that registered party members receive the party ballot based on the party indicated on his or her voter registration card. For example, in the Democratic primary, registered Democrats receive the Democratic ballot and choose from the Democratic candidates.

In primary elections, voters cast their vote by secret ballot in the privacy of a voting booth. In some states, however, primary

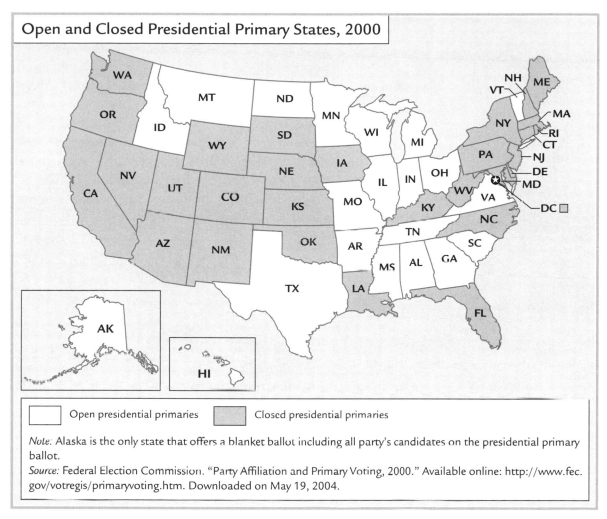

Open and Closed Presidential Primary States, 2000

☐ Open presidential primaries   ▨ Closed presidential primaries

Note: Alaska is the only state that offers a blanket ballot including all party's candidates on the presidential primary ballot.

Source: Federal Election Commission. "Party Affiliation and Primary Voting, 2000." Available online: http://www.fec.gov/votregis/primaryvoting.htm. Downloaded on May 19, 2004.

States determine how they will conduct their primary elections. Some choose to hold closed primaries, while others choose to hold open primaries. Alaska is the only state that offers a blanket ballot allowing any voter to vote for candidates of any party.

voters attend caucus meetings. This method of delegate selection includes open discussions and a public vote.

Caucuses

Instead of voting at the polls on a primary election day, voters in some states attend caucus meetings in each precinct where they divide into groups supporting each candidate. A great deal of discussion and persuasion may take place as the groups form. When

IOWA CAUCUSES

At the beginning of the 2004 election year, 36 states planned presidential primaries. The other 14 states and the District of Columbia planned to hold caucuses. Since 1963, when Iowa changed from primaries to caucuses, the Iowa caucus has become a tradition as the first event in each presidential primary. Although Iowa has only seven electoral votes, many political careers have ended when the candidate failed to place among the top three in the Iowa caucus. Other caucus candidates, however, have been hurled into the national spotlight. Media attention often increases donations that support a candidate's campaign in other state primaries. Consequently, the Iowa caucus is considered a way to gauge the candidates' potential to succeed in the general election.

all caucus attendees have joined a group supporting a candidate (or the group of uncommitted voters), the number of people in each group is counted. A mathematical formula is then used to determine how many delegates each group will select to support their candidate. The selected delegates attend the party's state convention. Delegates at the party's state convention decide which candidate's delegates will attend the party's national convention.

Selected in state primaries and caucuses, all the state delegates gather at the national convention to nominate the party's presidential candidate. Once the nominee is named, that candidate selects a vice presidential candidate. These two candidates run together on the party's president/vice president ticket, such as Kerry/Edwards on the Democratic ticket and Bush/Cheney on the Republican ticket in the 2004 election.

GENERAL ELECTION

The election of the president and vice president is the only national election in the United States. It is held in the years that divide evenly by four. Representatives and senators are elected in all even-numbered years, including the presidential election years.

The general election is the next-to-last vote in electing the president and vice president of the United States. After the popular vote (people's vote) has been counted to select the electors, several constitutional requirements and federal laws must be observed in completing the process of electing the president and vice president.

As soon as general election results are final, the governor of each state prepares seven originals of a document called "Certificates of Ascertainment." This document certifies the list of electors who will join the electors from the other states in electing the president and vice president. The states choose the format or design of the certificate; however, this legal document must be prepared and authenticated according to federal law. Each certificate must list the names of the electors the voters chose (the slate) and the number of votes the slate received. It must also list the names of all other candidates for elector (the losing parties' slates) and the number of votes each slate received. The governor must sign each certificate, and the state seal must be affixed to the document. One original and two certified copies of this document are sent to the archivist of the United States at the Office of the Federal Register as soon as possible. The legal staff of the Office of the Federal Register will examine the certificates. If all is in order, the certified copies are sent to the U.S. House of Representatives and the Senate. The other six originals will be attached to the Certificate of Vote after the electors have voted.

Electoral College

The states' electors meet on the Monday after the second Wednesday in December. This is the final step in the presidential election. The electors usually meet in their respective state capitols to cast each state's electoral vote. In accordance with the Constitution, the electors vote separate ballots for president and vice president.

There is no constitutional provision or federal law that requires electors to vote for the candidate who won the state's popular vote. The electors of 26 states and the District of Columbia are bound by state law to cast their vote for the candidate who won the state's popular vote. The other 24 can legally vote as they please. The political parties, however, take great care in choosing the individuals who serve as electors. They are usually hardworking activists who have demonstrated strong party loyalty. As a result, an elector almost never votes contrary to the state's popular vote.

"If the manner of it [electing the president] be not perfect, it is at least excellent."

—*Alexander Hamilton, Federalist No. 68, March 14, 1788*

After the electoral vote is cast, the electors prepare six "Certificates of Vote." Each certificate lists the name of the presidential and vice presidential candidate along with the number of electoral votes the candidates received. The six Certificates of Vote are paired with the remaining original Certificates of Ascertainment prepared earlier by the states and signed by one of their governors. The electors sign, seal, and certify the six packages of electoral votes. The packages are immediately sent to the president of the Senate, the archivist of the United States, and four other designated federal and state officials (state official titles and regulations vary).

The president of the Senate and other officials must receive the electoral votes by December 22. The presidential election process is complete when the president of the Senate counts the electoral vote before a joint session of Congress on January 6.

The U.S. Constitution requires that the president be elected by a majority of the electoral vote. There are 538 electoral votes, one for each member of the House of Representatives and Senate, with an additional three for the District of Columbia. This means that a presidential nominee must receive at least 270 electoral votes to be elected president. If no candidate receives a majority of the vote, the House of Representatives will determine the winner.

The electoral college is a complicated method of choosing the U.S. president and vice president. The founding fathers had two main concerns when they established this method for electing the president. First, they wanted to prevent the possibility that a tyrant could manipulate public opinion and be elected to the presidency. They believed that electors would be more knowledgeable about the workings of the government and the men (women could not vote or hold public office at that time) who were best qualified to fill the office. They thought the Electoral College would ensure that only a qualified person could be come president. Second, they believed that the Electoral College would assure a better balance between large and small states in the election of the president and vice president. States with the smallest population are assured at least three electoral votes, one for each senator and representative (each state has two senators and at least one representative). The Electoral College has withstood the test of time although controversy arises each time a president wins the electoral vote but loses the popular vote. This has occurred in the 1824, 1876, 1888, and 2000 elections.

CONGRESSIONAL AND OTHER ELECTIONS

The election of state governors, state legislators, and the U.S. House and Senate begins with a direct primary to choose candidates for office followed by an election. No electoral votes are involved; the

This 1913 political cartoon depicts the debate over direct primaries, which would move the nomination of candidates from congressional and legislative caucuses to a vote of the people. New York governor William Sulzer supported instituting direct primaries along with publisher William Randolph Hearst and former president Theodore Roosevelt. *(Library of Congress, Prints and Photographs Division [LC-USZ62-89418])*

"... our government is a government of the people. It was created by the people; it is sustained by the people; and the people are the government, to every political purpose and intent. And, in these consist the great and fundamental difference between a republican form of government and all others."

—*Ohio congressman Alexander Duncan, March 6, 1844*

people vote directly for these elected officials. This is called a direct election.

The U.S. Constitution created the legislative bodies of the U.S. government, including the House of Representatives and Senate. It also established the guidelines for the election of members of the U.S. Congress. According to the Constitution, members of the House were to be elected every two years by "the people of several states." The Constitution provided that the number of seats in the House would not exceed one representative for every 30,000 residents, based on a census taken every 10 years. If Congress had continued adding representatives at this rate, after the 1990 census the House would have 8,300 members. Fortunately, the founding fathers left Congress some options to make changes. Also, Congress had the foresight to pass the Permanent Apportionment Act in 1929, limiting the House to 435 seats, based on the 1910 census. Today, the 435 House seats are redivided among the states every 10 years based on growth and shifts in population and a complicated mathematical formula.

The Constitution also established that two senators would be elected by each state's legislature to serve six years. After the first election, the Constitution required that the Senate would be "divided as equally as may be into three Classes. The Seats of the Senators of the first Class shall be vacated at the Expiration of the second Year, of the second Class at the Expiration of the fourth Year, and of the third Class at the Expiration of the sixth Year, so that one third may be chosen every second Year." Thereafter, each Senate seat would come up for reelection every six years. According to this plan, one-third of the Senate seats comes up for reelection every two years. Today, members of the House and Senate are directly elected by the voters of each state.

Voters give senators and representatives the authority to represent them in the governing body that passes laws, levies taxes, and protects their interests. Although voters delegate this authority, they retain the power to change the government through the election process.

6

The Campaign Trail, the Media, and the Money

The Republican and Democratic Parties each have a solid base of party-line voters. Party-line voters, equal to about 30 percent of eligible voters, are those who vote for their party's candidates. This leaves about 40 percent of the eligible voters (swing voters) who may vote for any candidate. These voters decide how they will vote during the campaign. Many of them sway first toward one candidate and then toward the other. But, as with all voters, their decisions are not final until their ballot is cast. Consequently, the candidates begin to campaign months before the first presidential primary and stop on Election Day. During this time, each campaign spends time and money to influence the voters to favor its candidate over the opposition. In addition, each campaign works to strengthen the support of favorably decided voters while undermining support for an opponent.

On the campaign trail (the "path" politicians follow while campaigning for public office), the candidates running for election to a specific office campaign among the voters who have the authority and power to elect them. For example, city officials and mayors conduct their campaigns within city limits, and county officials stay within county boundaries. State legislators and U.S. representatives from each state campaign within their congressional districts. State governor and U.S. Senate candidates conduct statewide campaigns, and presidential candidates conduct national campaigns.

From the primaries to the national election, the campaign for U.S. president and vice president is the largest and most expensive in the world. It was not that way until the presidential election became partisan (involving support of a party or parties).

THE FOUNDING FATHERS' VIEW

The founding fathers did not mention political parties in the Constitution. They saw partisan factions (political parties) as a threat to the government that they were about to establish. Campaigning for lower-level offices within the states had long been partisan, and was sometimes wild, with food and liquor used to influence or reward voters on Election Day. The founding fathers agreed that the presidency should be kept nonpartisan and above this campaign fury. In their view, a man who possessed the character and stature to be president would have to be pressured to "stand for office." In other words, campaigning for president was thought to be beneath the dignity of a man worthy of the office. The common theory was that the office should seek the man; the man should not seek the office. Consequently, the first debates and presidential campaigns took place among legislators. Once the candidates were nominated, the next step was to convince each man selected to accept the nomination. The election then proceeded according to the guidelines set in the U.S. Constitution.

The first president of the United States, George Washington, upheld the idea that the presidency should be nonpartisan. Consequently, he chose men of diverse political views to serve in his cabinet. By the end of his first term, however, Washington's cabinet had divided into two factions that became the Federalist and the Democratic-Republican political parties. James Madison warned of the tendency to divide in 1787 when he participated in the Constitutional Convention:

A zeal for different opinions concerning religion, concerning government, and many other points . . . [has] divided mankind into parties, inflamed them with mutual animosity [hostility], and rendered them much more disposed to vex and oppress each other than to cooperate for their common good.

Once these political parties formed, the debate for the nomination of presidential candidates moved from the whole legislature to the factions within the legislature. In 1796, near the end of Washington's second term, at least 43 Democratic-Republican sen-

A BRIEF LOOK AT POLITICAL PARTIES

Believing that the executive branch of the U.S. government should remain nonpartisan, George Washington included men with a wide range of political views in his cabinet. The cabinet soon divided over foreign policy and the division of power between the federal government and the states.

Followers of Vice President John Adams and Secretary of the Treasury Alexander Hamilton believed in a strong federal government and a pro-British foreign policy. This group became known as Federalists.

Followers of Secretary of State Thomas Jefferson and prominent Virginian James Madison formed the Democratic-Republican Party. (They called themselves Republicans, but this party is not the Republican Party of today.) They wanted a limited federal government with little involvement in the state's economic affairs, and they leaned toward a pro-French foreign policy.

Once these political parties formed, others followed. Historians, however, identify every president, including George Washington, with a political party. Washington and John Adams were Federalists. Thomas Jefferson, James Monroe, and James Madison were Democratic-Republicans. These parties faded away. Andrew Jackson took office as a Democrat in 1829. He is considered the founder of the Democratic Party that exists today. (Today's Republican Party formed in 1854 to oppose the expansion of slavery and elected its first president, Abraham Lincoln, in 1860.)

Today the major parties, Republican and Democratic, oppose each other on almost all issues. Most voters identify themselves with one of these major parties, however, dozens of other parties (third parties) exist. Some of these parties were created to support or oppose an issue for a short time, and others have gained enough strength over time to nominate and elect candidates in local and state elections.

ators and representatives held a formal caucus to nominate Thomas Jefferson and Aaron Burr as the official party candidates. The Federalists also held a congressional nominating caucus. They chose John Adams and General Charles Cotesworth Pinckney as their candidates.

PARTISAN CONFLICT

A political free-for-all erupted in the presidential contest between Adams and Jefferson. Each candidate's supporters presented powerful arguments printed in newspapers, pamphlets, and delivered in speeches at political rallies. Democratic-Republican handbills praised Jefferson as a republican (supporting democracy) and depicted Adams as a monarchist who wanted to crown himself as king and ally the United States with its foe, Great Britain. Adams's supporters accused Jefferson of atheism (not believing in God), improper sexual conduct, and dangerous revolutionary intentions in support of France. Adams won the 1796 election, but Jefferson and Adams were nominated again in the 1800 election.

The 1800 election, however, did not go as the Democratic-Republicans planned. In an effort to elect Jefferson as president and Burr as vice president, the Democratic-Republican electors all voted for both men. Consequently, Jefferson and Burr received an equal number of electoral votes and tied for president. According to the Constitution, the tie was decided in the House of Representatives. The campaign continued in the House as members vigorously debated. They voted 36 times before Jefferson finally received the vote of 10 state delegations, giving him a majority of the vote. Burr received the vote of four states, making him vice president.

Throughout the campaign, Federalist leader Alexander Hamilton opposed Aaron Burr and frequently condemned him for being dangerous, ambitions, and unprincipled. In a letter to a fellow Federalist, Gouverneur Morris, Hamilton wrote, "Burr has no principle public or private . . . and will listen to no monitor but his ambition." Near the end of Burr's term as vice president, he entered the New York governor's race in the 1804 election. Hamilton continued his campaign against Burr. Some of Hamilton's derogatory remarks were made public in a newspaper. After Burr lost the election, he blamed Hamilton for his defeat. He considered his honor and reputation damaged by Hamilton's remarks. As sometimes happened when reputation was involved, Burr challenged Hamilton to a duel, and Hamilton had little choice but to accept the challenge. The two men faced each other in a formal duel on July 11, 1804. Hamilton's

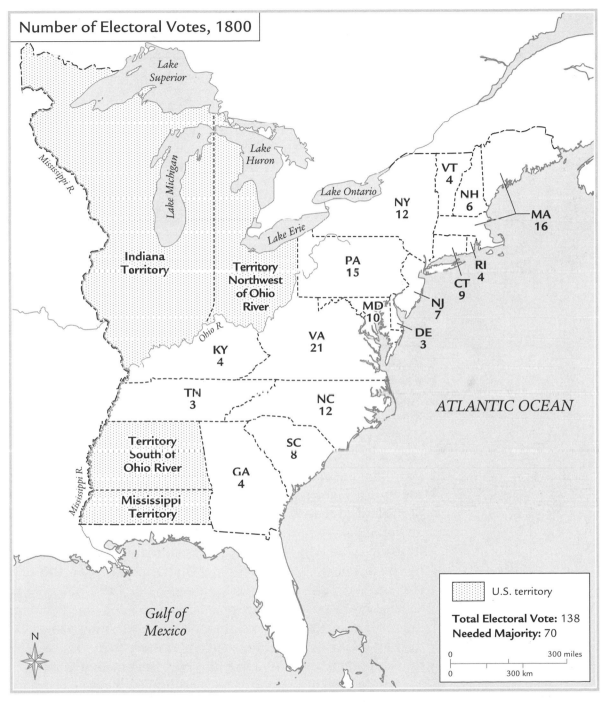

Number of Electoral Votes, 1800

Lake Superior

Lake Michigan

Lake Huron

Lake Ontario

Lake Erie

Mississippi R.

Indiana Territory

Territory Northwest of Ohio River

Ohio R.

KY 4

VA 21

PA 15

MD 10

NY 12

VT 4

NH 6

MA 16

RI 4

CT 9

NJ 7

DE 3

TN 3

NC 12

SC 8

GA 4

Territory South of Ohio River

Mississippi Territory

Mississippi R.

ATLANTIC OCEAN

Gulf of Mexico

N

U.S. territory

Total Electoral Vote: 138
Needed Majority: 70

0   300 miles

0   300 km

The map of the United States has changed since 1800. For example, North Carolina and Pennsylvania divided their electoral votes between two candidates in 1800. Today each state's electoral votes are awarded to one candidate (winner take all).

shot missed. Vice President Burr's found its target and inflicted a mortal wound. Hamilton died the next day, and the vice president of the United States was charged with murder. The case was not prosecuted, and Burr served out his term as vice president.

Efforts to influence voters, from that time until this, have brought hot debate laced with scathing accusations based on selected facts that may distort the facts. Then as now, the truth is hard to determine, and what voters choose to believe determines the election outcome. The Hamilton/Burr conflict, however, is the only one (thus far) that resulted in an exchange of bullets, death, and murder charges.

THE CANDIDATE ON THE CAMPAIGN TRAIL

Through the last half of the 19th century, presidential nominees slowly began to emerge as candidates who campaigned for themselves. William Henry Harrison was the first presidential candidate to go on the campaign trail. Harrison focused attention on his experience as a former army officer who had battled the Shawnee at Tippecanoe Creek in Indiana Territory. This battle and those that followed led to the opening of the northwestern frontier to white settlement. Harrison, known as "Old Tip," used this military experience as an excuse to make a speaking tour through Indiana and Illinois in summer 1835. He entertained crowds with war stories during the annual anniversary celebration of the battle of Tippecanoe. The press glorified Harrison's military career (almost 25 years in the past) and promoted him as a possible presidential nominee. The publicity secured the Whig Party's presidential nomination for Harrison, but his opponent Martin Van Buren (a Democrat) won the 1836 election and became the eighth president of the United States. Undaunted, Harrison began openly campaigning for the Whig nomination in 1840. By now, the 67-year-old Harrison was an old man by standards of the time. Still, after more than four years on the campaign trail Harrison won the Whig nomination.

His Democratic opponents, supporting Van Buren for a second term, referred to Old Tip as Granny, implied he was senile, and belittled his military career. For example, a writer for a Democratic newspaper wrote, "Give him a barrel of hard cider and settle a pension of two thousand a year on him, and [take] my word for it he will sit . . . by the side of a 'sea coal' fire, and study moral philosophy."

The Harrison campaign turned this intended insult into a memorable campaign strategy. Harrison had lived on the frontier while fighting and negotiating treaties with the Indians. He was born on a plantation, privately tutored, and studied medicine before deciding on a military career. The campaign, however, focused on his frontier days, presenting him to the voters as a simple frontier Indian fighter who lived in a log cabin and drank cider. At the same time, the Harrison campaign portrayed Van Buren as a rich, champagne-sipping aristocrat. Harrison became the "log cabin" (not privileged) candidate. (In fact, a log cabin background continued to be important to presidential candidates until 1860, when Abraham Lincoln was elected.)

THE POLITICAL DANCING JACK:
A Holiday Gift for Sucking Whigs!!

Although William Henry Harrison campaigned for himself, the Whig and Democrat parties were locked in a fierce battle in support of their candidates. This Democrat campaign cartoon shows two influential Whigs, Senator Henry Clay (left) and Congressman Henry A. Wise, operating a "dancing Jack" puppet that strongly resembles Harrison. *(Library of Congress, Prints and Photographs Division [LC-USZ62-14982])*

Political advisers told Harrison to keep his lips sealed on the controversial issues, including slavery, the tariff, and the U.S. bank. Tales of Harrison's military experience dazzled voters and distracted them from his avoidance of the issues. Whig Party leaders named John Tyler, a former Virginia senator, as the vice presidential candidate. The catchy slogan "Tippecanoe and Tyler, too" linked the military hero and the southern senator, thus appealing to voters in the South as well as the North. Harrison won the 1840 election and became the ninth president of the United States. He served only one month before he died of pneumonia. Although he served the shortest term, he had an impact on the nation as the first presidential candidate to actively campaign to gain votes for himself.

Harrison campaigned while his opponent (Van Buren) remained presidential and silent. Through the next few elections, some candidates chose to follow Harrison's path while others chose to remain "presidential" and silent. Often, the campaigning candidate lost the

RADIO AND TELEVISION CHANGE THE COURSE OF POLITICAL CAMPAIGNS

Radio: In 1992, Warren Harding (the 29th president) was the first president to make a live broadcast. His speech at the dedication of the Francis Scott Key Memorial was broadcast by station WEAR in Baltimore, Maryland.

Three years later, in 1925, Calvin Coolidge (a Republican and the 30th U.S. president) delivered the first live broadcast presidential inaugural speech.

Franklin Delano Roosevelt (a Democrat and the 32nd U.S. president) made weekly radio broadcasts he called Fireside Chats beginning in 1933. These weekly messages created a personal relationship between Roosevelt and the American people. This frequent contact, plus the success of his policies and programs, won the approval of the voters who elected him to four terms in office. (Roosevelt died April 12, 1945, in the first year of his fourth term.)

Television: By 1952, television stations were spread across the nation, and many American homes had television sets. That year, Dwight D. Eisenhower (Republican) and Adlai Stevenson (Democrat) were the first presidential candidates to use television adver-

election. It would be some time before the American electorate completely gave up the notion that "the office should seek the man."

TRANSPORTATION AND COMMUNICATION

The Democratic Party gained power and dominated politics through the first half of the 1800s. The Republican Party rose out of the ashes of the Whigs' demise after Harrison's election. The party gained power in the 1850s and Abraham Lincoln, its candidate, was elected president in 1860. Since that time, U.S. politics has been basically a two-party system with Democratic and Republican candidates battling each other for the White House. Other parties have nominated candidates, but no third-party presidential candidate has won.

From horse-and-buggy days, to radio, the railroad, television, and the digital age, advances in technology have progressively changed the campaign trail.

tising. In addition, the 1952 Republican and Democratic conventions were televised.

In 1960, as the television audience watched, presidential candidates Richard M. Nixon (Republican) and John F. Kennedy (Democrat) participated in the first televised presidential debate. The changes television would bring to political campaigns became clear. Most people who heard the debate on radio liked Nixon's stand on the issues. Listeners thought Nixon won. Many people who saw the debate on television judged the debate on the candidates' appearance. Kennedy looked youthful and confident while Nixon looked tired and disgruntled. Viewers thought Kennedy won. Since that time, a candidate's appearance has steadily gained importance in political campaigns. William Jefferson Clinton (a Democrat and the 42nd president) used Hollywood advisers, hairdressers, and makeup artists during his campaigns and presidency. Albert Gore (2000 Democratic presidential candidate) included a wardrobe expert and image analyst among his campaign advisers. In the 20th century a voter-pleasing, photogenic television appearance became a campaign must, and this has continued into the 21st century.

> "I have been assailed so bitterly that I hardly knew whether I was running for the presidency or the penitentiary."
>
> —*Horace Greeley, defeated in the 1872 presidential campaign*

Franklin D. Roosevelt was the first U.S. president to fly. Obviously enjoying the flight over the Atlantic, Roosevelt studies a map with Captain Otis Bryan. *(Library of Congress, Prints and Photographs Division, Official U.S. Navy Photo from O.W.I. [LC-USZ62-97736])*

Radio brought voices of sitting presidents into the American home. Although Warren Harding and Calvin Coolidge made occasional radio speeches, Franklin D. Roosevelt was the first to establish frequent contact with the public in his Fireside Chats. Roosevelt also toured the nation by train, setting a record for train travel: 243,827 miles. For almost 100 years, U.S. presidents had traveled by train. By the mid-1940s, however, times and transportation were changing. In 1944, President Roosevelt ordered the creation of the Presidential Pilot Office to provide air transportation to the president and his staff. Roosevelt's plane, a Douglas C-54 called the *Sacred Cow,* was built in 1944 with a specially designed interior and an elevator to lift the president in his wheelchair in and out of the plane. This four-engine propeller-driven plane served through the Truman administration (1945–53). The first *Air Force One* jet was christened during the Eisenhower administration (1953–61).

Although advancing technology has changed some aspects of political campaigns, the age-old campaign strategy remains the same: Promote one candidate and degrade (destroy) the others. Politics is war, and all is fair. What the voters believe on Election Day will determine the election. Candidates, their campaign staff, and supporters work very hard to mold and manipulate the voters' beliefs during the campaign. Each campaign presents its candidate in the best light while casting shadows of suspicion and doubt on the other candidates.

Today, the presidential campaign is a daily news event brought into almost every American home by network and cable news. News organizations compete for viewers and readers while the candidates compete for voters. Scandals and personal attacks attract a bigger audience than a presentation of each candidate's program and achievements. Good press is priceless, but bad press can be costly. News coverage is free and campaigns vie to capture it by staging events that the media will want to cover. Candidates and

"When your opponent is on the air, you can't let it go unanswered for long."

—*Rick Lazio, former U.S. Representative from New York, March 21, 2001*

their supporters also spend millions of dollars on political ads to influence voters. Many of these ads discredit the opponents' record and political promises while others redirect bad press and defend against the opponents' attack ads (known as damage control).

The Media

The mass media—including major newspapers, network and cable television, and radio—receive a large portion of each presidential candidate's campaign money. In fact, mass media advertising is considered to have such an influence on voters that political analysts commonly project that the candidate who raises the most money to spend on advertising will win an election. It is hard to determine, however, whether candidates win because they raise the most money or they raise the most money because they have more support. Adequate money to run a campaign is a must, and the cost of campaigning climbs higher with every election. For example, in the 1996 presidential campaign, the major party candidates, William Clinton and Robert Dole, spent a combined $232 million. Four years later, George Bush and Albert Gore spent a combined total of $306 million.

Opinion Polls

Candidates and political parties want to know how their campaigns are going and what issues should be addressed in future ads and speeches. Political parties and candidates set up phone banks to poll selected groups, usually those most likely to vote. Paid workers and political volunteers telephone voters, asking them questions to determine which issues are important and which candidate would win if the election were held today. Political parties and candidates compile this information and use the results to alter campaign strategies and focus campaign advertising. Each campaign addresses the issues most likely to influence voters in its favor. The 1990s, however, introduced a new method of communication on the campaign trail.

The Internet

The Internet became a significant campaign tool in the Clinton years. Political scientist Bruce Bimber, associate professor of political science at the University of California at Santa Barbara, analyzed how candidates used the Internet in the 2000 presidential election. He found that Web sites did not help undecided voters make their

> "We believe electronic word-of-mouth is the best form of voter contact. It's personalized, it's targeted and it works with lightning speed."
>
> —Larry Purpuro, George W. Bush's deputy chief of staff for 2000 campaign, quoted in the New York Times, November 11, 2000

CAMPAIGN FINANCE REFORM

When the nation was new, elected officials were men of wealth. They often secured votes by rewarding voters with food and drink. In time, the growth of the nation increased the government workforce and offered more opportunity for political reward. Government jobs were considered the spoils of the campaign, and newly elected officials replaced most of the government workers under their control with supporters who had contributed to their campaigns. Henry Clay observed that after an election government workers from the outgoing administration were "like the inhabitants of Cairo when the plague breaks out; no one knows who is next to encounter the stroke of death." Many of the individuals appointed to these government jobs lacked the skills needed to perform the positions they filled. Efficiency suffered and corruption flourished.

Congress tackled this problem by passing the Pendleton Act in 1883. This act intended to end the "spoils system" of campaign finance and improve the quality of government workers. It created the Civil Service merit system, which required that applicants pass the appropriate tests before being considered for government jobs. As a result, government workers gained employment by their own merit. Still, Congress left some opportunity for rewarding campaign workers and contributors. Some higher-level positions were held outside the merit system to be filled by political appointment.

From that time on, as the need for campaign funds constantly increased, Congress passed other legislation intended to control campaign financing. However, members of Congress themselves had campaigns to finance. Consequently, legal scrutiny always revealed loopholes that provided a path for acquiring donations from wealthy contributors expecting rewards. As a result, large corporations and labor unions have continuously gained election influence, leaving government officials vulnerable to corruption.

In 2000, Senator John McCain (Republican–Arizona) campaigned in the primary for nomination as the party's presiden-

decisions. Instead, Web sites proved to be more useful in strengthening the loyalty of the candidate's supporters. According to Bimber, "People tend to go to the Web sites of the candidates they

tial candidate. He supported campaign finance reform and made this one of his main issues. After losing his bid for the nomination, McCain returned to the Senate. McCain and fellow senator Russell Feingold (Democrat–Wisconsin) worked together to create a bill designed to reform federal campaign finance laws. The Senate passed the Bipartisan Campaign Reform Act of 2002 (known as the McCain-Feingold Law) on March 20, 2002, and President George W. Bush signed it into law on March 27, 2002. The changes to the federal campaign finance laws were scheduled to take effect on November 6, after the 2002 election.

The McCain-Feingold Law prohibits national parties and federal candidates from raising and spending money from corporations and labor unions. In addition, the act increases the amount individuals can donate to candidates and political parties. The intent of these changes is to decrease the political influence of corporations and labor unions and increase the influence of individual voters.

Opponents of the McCain-Feingold Law challenged the law in the U.S. Supreme Court in a landmark case known as *McConnell v. Federal Election Commission*. On December 10, 2003, the Court issued a decision that declared all major provisions of the law constitutional.

Still, a loophole was found. Certain nonprofit organizations can legally raise and spend unlimited amounts of money for elections as long as these nonprofits are separate from any candidate of a political party. In the 2004 presidential election, 527 nonprofit organizations, such as Vietnam Vets for Truth and MoveOn.org, raised massive amounts of money for both major party candidates. The 527 organizations used this money to buy television time for political ads that subtly supported a particular candidate without actually mentioning voting for that candidate. As a result, these organizations bypassed the intent of the McCain-Feingold Law and unregulated campaign spending soared.

support, and they tend to come away feeling even more strongly about them than they did going in."

The Internet also provides campaigns with quick communication through e-mail. By the 2004 election, e-mail capabilities had increased to include film clips that looked much like television ads sent via the Internet. These mass e-mail mailings deliver the candidate's message to a targeted recipient at a very low cost. E-mail also allows the recipient to read the message at a convenient time. The message can then be forwarded to friends with a few clicks of the mouse. Internet campaign costs include software and personnel to design and produce the Web site and campaign material to be distributed in e-mail. The cost of producing and maintaining a Web site for a national campaign in the 2004 election reached more than $1 million. This is a minimal expense, however, in a budget that may reach more than $300 million.

MONEY

Campaign spending increased dramatically from the first Republican/Democratic race in 1860 to the 2000 election. The Abraham Lincoln campaign spent $150,000, the equivalent of less than $4 million in 2000 dollars. The George W. Bush campaign spent almost $186 million in the 2000 election. Expenses for the 2004 Bush reelection campaign reached $306 million. It is easy to see that potential candidates and incumbents (those in office who plan to seek another term) must devote a massive amount of time of fund-raising.

After taking office, the sitting president who plans to become the incumbent candidate must continue fund-raising throughout the first four-year term. Although many fund-raising events are held by the political parties, the most effective events feature a speech by the presidential candidate. As a result, the president and his challenger attend many expensive dinners and events, where people likely to make large donations are present. However, millions of individual supporters send small amounts of money to the campaign as the result of fund-raising letters and e-mail asking for their support.

This money is spent in many ways, including for campaign staff, transportation, hotels, food, polling, voter registration, and mass media advertising. All of it is used to influence the voters, encourage more voters to register, and motivate them all go to the polls on Election Day.

7

To the Polls!

The voters go to the polls (voting places) to cast their votes on Election Day. Casting a vote in a local, state, or national election is an official act that determines who will run the local, state, and federal government and how it will be run. This is the power of the vote that is protected by each state in the election process.

As colonies and territories became states, each new state adopted a state constitution. Provisions of those constitutions defined how elections would be conducted and who would have the right to vote. Election precincts and the duties of election officials (usually election judges) were established. In a speech to the House of Representatives in 1944, Ohio representative Alexander Duncan explained the duties of election judges: "whose duty is to know of themselves, or by information, all persons who are or are not entitled the use of the elective franchise [vote]. The judges are sworn to receive no vote from the hand of any one not entitled to a vote within the precinct, and to reject all votes from persons living without the precinct, whether citizens of the State or the United States, or not." In the early days of the Republic, judges knew "of themselves" (knew personally) who was entitled to vote and who was not. As the population grew, however, the job became more difficult. They needed to have the information gathered and prepared for them before the election. When judges could no longer identify qualified voters from their own knowledge, state legislatures began considering better ways to identify qualified voters.

STATES ADOPT VOTER REGISTRATION

Massachusetts, the first state to take action, began requiring the assessor of every town or plantation to prepare lists of qualified voters. Oral applications for new registration were heard the day before an election. These new voters were added to the rolls from previous elections and a revised registration list was posted on Election Day before the voting began.

Voter registration was adopted throughout New England by 1860. Most of the northern states began registering voters from

---

A LITTLE HISTORY

When the United States was new, elections were conducted much as they had been in England, "on the voices." Voters gathered at local centers, such as the town square or village green. The election was conducted by a local official, such as the sheriff. Each voter stepped forward in turn and spoke the name of his chosen candidate. The votes were tallied, similar to scoring a game or sports event. This public voting could make the voter vulnerable to bribery and intimidation.

After the two-party system emerged, printed ballots replaced the voice vote. Each major party printed colored tickets listing the party candidates. As voters marked their ballot, observers knew how they voted by the color of their ballot. This system also left the voter open to bribery and intimidation.

The secret ballot (first used in Australia in 1856) helped prevent bribery and voter intimidation. The secret ballot system includes a voting booth and preprinted ballots similar to the paper ballots used in many countries today. All candidates are listed on the ballot. The voter marks his or her choice in private (secret) and places it in a sealed ballot box. When the ballots are removed to be counted, no one can know how anyone voted. New York began using the "Australian ballot" in 1889, and other states soon followed. In 1892, Grover Cleveland was the first U.S. president elected after the secret ballot came into use.

**NORTH DAKOTA
ABOLISHED VOTER REGISTRATION IN 1951**

This sparsely populated state staffs its polling places with a precinct election board and political-party poll challengers who know everyone who lives in their district. These election officials are authorized to challenge any person at the polls whom they suspect is not qualified to vote in the precinct. The challenged person is asked to show evidence that he or she is a U.S. citizen, at least 18 years old, and a legal North Dakota resident living in the precinct for at least 30 days preceding the election. In addition, the person must not have been declared mentally incompetent or convicted of a felony unless his or her rights have been restored. The person may be asked to sign an affidavit stating that he or she is qualified to vote in North Dakota. The information on the affidavit will verified. Any suspected violations will be brought to the attention of the county auditor and county state's attorney for investigation and possible prosecution. Falsely swearing to be a qualified voter in North Dakota is a class A misdemeanor with a maximum penalty of one year in prison and/or a fine of $2,000. After signing the affidavit, the person is allowed to vote. The voter's eligibility will be verified before the ballot is counted.

1860 to 1880, and the policy spread through the South and West from 1880 to 1900. Each state determined its own form of registration and qualifications for voting.

Today, 49 states and the District of Columbia require voter registration. Only North Dakota has no registration requirement. In all other states, eligible citizens must meet state voting requirements and register to vote a certain length of time before the next election. The registration is valid as long as all the information submitted on the registration card remains unchanged.

State Requirements

Some states have a long list of voting requirements while others have only a few. Massachusetts, for example, has three basic requirements plus a registration deadline: Voters must be U.S.

citizens, 18 years old by Election Day, live in Massachusetts, and register at least 20 days before the next primary or general election (10 days before a special town meeting). Most other states add requirements to these basics. Most states deny voter registration to convicted felons who are serving prison terms, but most reinstate voting rights after the convicted felon has served his or her term and is no longer on parole. (Florida does not.) Most states do not allow people to register to vote who have been declared mentally incompetent by a judge. In addition, all states must comply with federal laws and constitutional amendments that forbid denying the vote to anyone over age 18 based on race or gender.

Registering to Vote

Most states require the completion of a voter registration form. Information required on the form includes full name, current address, and date of birth. Some states require a choice of political party. To complete the registration form, the voter must sign a statement swearing that he or she is a citizen of the United States who meets the state requirements to vote and that all the information he or she provided on the registration form is true. Making false statements on a voter registration card is a federal and state crime punishable by a prison term and/or fine.

Comparing U.S. census results with voter registration numbers indicates that many eligible voters are not registered. In the mid-1990s, Congress passed a law that it thought would make voter registration more convenient.

National Voter Registration Act

The National Voter Registration Act made voter registration much easier for everyone. Congress passed this act, also called the Motor Voter Law, in 1993 and it became effective nationwide on January 1, 1995.

After that time, citizens could register to vote at their state's Department of Motor Vehicles when they applied for a driver's license or vehicle registration. In addition, registration was offered at government public assistance offices and armed forces recruitment centers. People registering at these sites could also receive assistance in filling out the registration form.

In accordance with the National Voter Registration Act, a national voter registration form was created that can be printed from the Internet (http://www.fec.gov/votregis/pdf/nvra.pdf). After the printed form is filled out and signed, it can be mailed to the appropriate office of the state where the voter lives. The person's name is placed on the voting roll as soon as the form is received and accepted in the proper state office. New Hampshire and Wyoming, however, do not accept the national form, and each state's form must be requested.

Qualified U.S. citizens can register at any time. In order for a person to participate in the next election, the registration form must reach the proper office before the state's deadline. In most states, the deadline is 10 to 30 days before the coming election. This gives county officials time to prepare the precinct rolls that the poll workers will use to identify registered voters as they arrive at the polls.

President Bill Clinton signs the National Voter Registration Act of 1993 as Vice President Al Gore and several members of Congress look on. *(Library of Congress, Prints and Photographs Division, official White House photograph [LC-USZ62-113154])*

POLL WORKERS

Poll workers staff the polls during every election. Their job is to assure that only registered voters receive a ballot and to conduct fair and honest elections. In the early 1800s, poll workers relied mostly on their own knowledge. Today, voter registration information is recorded in a book that is present in the precinct polls before the first voter arrives on Election Day.

In most states, three to five poll workers are needed in every precinct on Election Day. County election officials select or appoint and train these workers in some states. In Pennsylvania, however, each election district (precinct) elects an election district board every four years. The members of this board include a judge of elections, a majority inspector (representing the major political party in the majority at the local level) and a minority inspector (representing the other major party). In addition to the three-member board, the poll is also attended by two poll watchers for each candidate and three from each party. Miami-Dade County in Florida staffs its polls with a clerk, assistant clerk, an inspector, and a deputy sheriff. The deputy stands outside the polling place to maintain peace. Some states have chief and assistant chief election officers. Others have precinct judges and clerks. Both major parties are represented at the polls. No matter what title is used, however, all these poll workers work 14 hours or more on Election Day to ensure that elections are run in an honest and organized manner.

In most states, payment varies from about $5.00 to $11.00 per hour depending on the duties of the poll worker. On election morning, poll workers must be at their assigned polling place one hour before the polls open. The poll worker who is in charge of the poll brings the precinct roll and other materials, including paper ballots, to the polling place on Election Day. If voting machines are used, the county office arranges for delivery to the site. If computer equipment is used, technicians accompany the machines to the site and remain there throughout the day. Poll workers are instructed to bring lunch. They cannot leave the polling place until their work is done.

THE POLLS

The polls are temporarily set up in existing establishments for use on Election Day. The location must be convenient to most resi-

This 1857 political cartoon depicts differences in strong political opinions leading to physical violence at the polls. Today polling places are usually peaceful as a result of laws prohibiting campaigning near the polls on Election Day. *(Library of Congress, Prints and Photographs Division [LC-USZ62-118012])*

dents of the precinct and able to accommodate a steady trail of voters as they come and go. In small precincts, a room in a home may be volunteered to serve as a polling place. Most polls, however, are set up in public buildings, such as a school, community center, or church. These public facilities are usually accessible to handicapped voters.

The polls must occupy only one room and all parts of that room must be visible to all poll workers. The room must be big enough so that no one comes within 10 feet of the voters in the voting booths. This protects the secrecy of the ballot and prevents overzealous activists from trying to influence voters as they make their final decisions.

EARLY VOTING IN TEXAS

Election officials have been concerned about the low voter turnout in recent elections. In an attempt to increase turnout by making voting easier, Texas adopted the Early Voting program in the mid-1990s. This program provides voters an opportunity to vote at their convenience within the last two weeks before an election. In the Early Voting two-week period, however, voters can choose any of the Early Polling places in their county. This means that instead of rushing home to vote before their precinct polls close on Election Day, voters can choose to vote on their lunch hour near their office, for example. Voters must present identification such as a voter registration card, valid Texas driver's license, or state identification card. Using the name and address on the identification material, poll workers verify the voter's registration on a database.

Texas voting officials estimate that 25 to 30 percent of voters in each election take advantage of Early Voting. As a result of this success, several other states have followed Texas's lead and adopted an Early Voting program.

ABSENTEE BALLOTS

Voting an absentee ballot is another way to make voting easier for some voters. Originally, the absentee ballot protected the rights of vacationers and military personnel stationed around the world as well as the handicapped. Today, in some states, such as California and Arizona, the absentee ballot is used to make voting easier for anyone who wants to use it; no reason is needed. Any registered voter can request an absentee ballot and vote when it is most convenient. Other states, such as New York and Massachusetts, however, still restrict absentee voting to voters who are away from home or physically unable to go to the polls.

A voter can request an absentee ballot two to three weeks before an election in most states. (This time frame varies according to state requirements.) The completed ballot must be placed in the official envelope provided with the ballot. This envelope has an official form on the outside that must be completed and signed by the voter. The envelope may be mailed or delivered in person to the polls or county election office. It must be postmarked on or before Election Day or arrive before the polls close on Election Day.

Before the envelope is opened, the information in the outside form is checked and the signature is compared to the voter's signature on his or her registration card. If all is in order, the envelope is opened, and the ballot is then removed and added to other ballots ready to be counted.

HELP AMERICA VOTE ACT

After the 2000 presidential election, the accuracy and security of the punch-card ballot came into question. As a result, Congress passed the Help America Vote Act of 2001 (HAVA). President George W. Bush signed it into law in October 2002. In part, the legislation was designed to make the voting process easier for handicapped voters. It was mainly designed, however, to eliminate the problems Florida and other states encountered with vote-counting machines in the 2000 presidential election. Most of these problems involved punch-card voting systems. Some people found the ballots confusing and punched a hole for more than one presidential candidate. Others failed to punch the prescored square completely from the ballot. This left a "hanging chad" attached to the ballot that confused the vote-counting machine. The machine rejected these improperly punched ballots and did not count those votes. HAVA called for the replacement of all the trouble-prone systems by the November 2004 general elections. States that could offer good reason for delaying this deadline could request a waiver extending the deadline to January 1, 2006. The legislation included $3.8 billion in federal aid to help states purchase new voting machines.

ELECTRONIC VOTING

By the time HAVA went into effect, electronic voting machines were already available and in use in several states. With the market suddenly expanded, more companies scrambled to produce an electronic voting machine that would better meet the demand of HAVA: one that is easy for all people to use and produces a quick, accurate vote count. Some states adopted "direct recording electronic" (DRE) voting systems in 2002. With some of these machines, the voter makes his or her selection by touching the screen. On others, a knob or wheel is turned to highlight the candidate's name before making the selection.

As is often the case with new technology, many people are concerned about the integrity and security of the electronic voting machines. According to Congressman Dennis Kucinich (Democrat–Ohio) "The problem with the [DRE] voting system is that [the] entire election relies on the strength, accuracy, and security of the software used in the voting terminal, all three of which have since shown severe flaws."

Another form of electronic voting, casting votes on the Internet, has been tried but not readily accepted. Many computer experts believe that software used in Internet voting as well as electronic voting machines can be hacked and altered. Votes can be changed or additional votes can be cast with a few clicks of a mouse. Thus the outcome of an election can be manipulated.

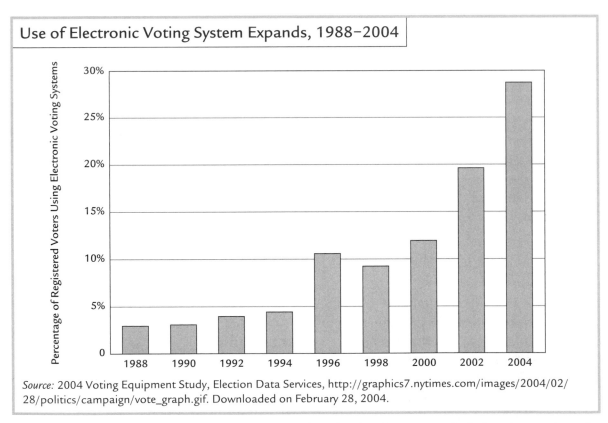

Use of Electronic Voting System Expands, 1988–2004

Source: 2004 Voting Equipment Study, Election Data Services, http://graphics7.nytimes.com/images/2004/02/28/politics/campaign/vote_graph.gif. Downloaded on February 28, 2004.

The Help America Vote Act required the replacement of outdated voting systems, including the punch-card ballot and pull-lever voting machines. Still, by 2004, less than 30 percent of voters cast their ballots on electronic voting machines.

Most experts agree that the ability to verify the vote with a paper record would provide the necessary security. Douglas Jones, a University of Iowa computer science professor serving on the Iowa board of examiners for electronic voting systems, told a reporter, "If you have [a] voter-verifiable audit trail [paper record], even the devil himself could design the software, and you'd still be able to conduct an honest election."

Most people have enough confidence in electronic security to do their banking on the Internet, by phone, and with automated teller machines. In addition, many people shop online, billing their purchase to their credit cards with little concern. These actions indicate confidence in Internet and electronic security. If security for the voting process can be proven, Internet and electronic voting (and counting) will likely gain general acceptance.

"All online voting will do is give us a very clear indication of who the hackers want to be president."

—Eric Bangeman, remembering the words of a college instructor in 2000, Ars Technical Newsdesk Web site, January 22, 2004

8

Tallying the Vote

In most states, each county is responsible for choosing and purchasing voting equipment. As a result, an assortment of voting machines may be used within one state. The voting method used at the polls determines how the canvass (count) will be conducted. Some voting systems tally each vote as it is cast. Others require securing the ballot boxes and taking them to a central counting center.

The plan in every election is that every ballot will be carefully examined and every vote will be counted. No canvassing method has proven to be completely accurate, and some votes are lost in every election. Sometimes the voter is at fault; sometimes the canvass method fails to count some ballots. The number of errors, however, is seldom enough to change the outcome of an election.

In more than two centuries of elections, the canvassing process has changed with the times. It has moved from relying on human skill, to mechanical systems, to computers and the digital age. These changes have been necessary as the electorate expanded and the number of ballots to process increased. For example, in the 1824 election, little more than 262,000 votes were tallied for the two main presidential candidates; in the 2000 election, this number exceeded 101 million. Furthermore, the increasing population required more government services and the election of more local and state officials. Consequently, ballots had more items to mark and count. As a result, election officials had to look for a better way to tally the vote.

PULL-LEVER
VOTE-COUNTING MACHINE

Jacob H. Myers invented the first vote-counting machine in the late 1800s. Myers said he designed this machine to "protect mechanically the voter from rascaldom [mischief], and make the process of casting the ballot perfectly plain, simple and secret." Lockport, New York, tested Myers's pull-lever machine in the 1892 election. Rochester, New York, used it citywide in 1894, and the machine was widely used in the state of New York within a few years. By the 1950s, improved versions of Myers's vote counting machine had been adopted throughout the United States. These machines presented the ballot by assigning each candidate and ballot question a specific lever on the face of the machine. The voter, hidden behind a curtain, indicated his or her choices by pulling the appropriate lever to the down position.

This 1927 photo shows the security involved in transporting ballot boxes from the polls to the canvassing center. Note that the boxes are sealed and two officials are involved in identifying and recording receipt of the boxes. *(Library of Congress, Prints and Photographs Division, National Photo Company Collection [LC-USZ62-110529])*

"From a legal perspective, a ballot is an instrument, just like a deed or check. When the ballot is deposited in the ballot box, it becomes anonymous, but just prior to the moment when the ballot is deposited, it ought to be possible to hand the ballot to the voter and ask 'Does this ballot properly represent your intent?'"

—*Douglas W. Jones, associate professor of computer science, University of Iowa, at the annual meeting of the League of Women Voters of Johnson County, Iowa City, Iowa, May 16, 2001*

When the voter pulled the handle that opened the curtain, the vote was recorded as the levers returned to the original position.

VOTE COUNTING

When the democratic republic was new, the vote was tallied as it was cast. There were no ballots and no ballot boxes. Each voter stood before the voting official and announced his vote in public. As the word was uttered, the vote was counted. People gathered at any polling place could hear every vote and see it counted—the vote was as public as points scored at a ball game. The vote was easy to tally as long as only adult white male property owners could vote and a good turnout brought only 20 or 30 voters to a polling place.

The ability to count votes as they were cast ended when each political party began printing a list of the party's candidates on colored paper. This was called the party ticket, such as the Democrat ticket or the Whig ticket. Since most voters simply dropped a party ticket in the ballot box, votes could be hand counted by sorting the tickets according to color.

The adoption of the secret ballot, with candidates from all parties printed on one ballot, further slowed the counting process. Hand counting required careful examination of every ballot, reading candidates' names, marking the voter's choices on a tally sheet, and counting marks. In tallying the vote, a mark (such as the numeral 1) was made in each candidate's column for each vote received. To make the counting easier, four marks crossed through with one diagonal line (卌) equaled five votes. An accurate count required an honest counter plus the deposit of only one ballot per voter in the ballot box.

Reports of election fraud soon surfaced. Some vote counters were accused of adding votes to their favorite candidate's column, and some voters were suspected of adding ballots to the ballot boxes. People who believed that paper ballots and hand counting allowed opportunity for election fraud welcomed the invention of the pull-lever vote-counting machines in the late 1800s.

This voter has just cast his vote on a pull-lever vote-counting machine. As soon as he pulled the lever to open the curtain, the machine recorded his vote. *(Library of Congress, United States Office of War Information [LC-USW3-055964-D])*

After the polls closed, poll workers read and recorded the total vote for each candidate and question from a counter on each machine. The mechanical counter looked something like an odometer on an old car. In the event of a close election, however, a recount was not possible because no paper ballots were used in these machines.

The count tallied by the machine was the only record of the vote. Consequently, the election was only as honest as the mechanic who kept the voting machine in working order. The mechanic could alter the way the machine counted the votes, skipping a few for one party's candidates and adding some for the other party.

Some people believed that the pull-lever voting machine without a paper ballot offered too much opportunity for election fraud.

> "Punch card machines belong in the Smithsonian, not in a United States voting booth."
>
> —*Congressman Bob Ney (Republican–Ohio), cosponsor of Help America Vote Act, 2002*

They welcomed the introduction of the punch-card ballot in the 1960s.

PUNCH-CARD BALLOT

The punch-card ballot has rows of small pre-scored squares. A specific square represents each candidate and ballot question on the ballot. When the card is inserted in the punch-card voting machine (about the size of a clipboard), the edge of each page of ballot questions lines up with a column of holes that align with a column of squares on the punch card. The voter makes his or her selection by inserting a stylus (pin) in the designated hole and forcing it through the pre-scored square on the ballot. The small square (chad) falls from the punch card, leaving a hole. During the canvass, the cards are fed into a counting machine that "reads" the holes and counts the votes.

The close presidential election in 2000 and the Florida recount called attention to faults with the punch-card counting process.

For various reasons, some punches on some ballots are not counted in almost every county in almost every election where punch cards are used. This can happen if the voter fails to punch the chad completely from the card or punches two candidates for the same office. Since this is usually a random occurrence, with most candidates losing or gaining a few votes, it seldom changes the outcome of an election. Still, when the tally is within a few hundred votes, the losing candidate hopes to pick up more votes than the other candidate in a recount of punch-card ballots.

Many problems developed in the 2000 presidential election recount. No one wanted a repeat of this election crisis, and Congress passed the Help America Vote Act requiring replacement of punch-card and pull-lever voting machines. The optical-scan vote-counting process was one acceptable system.

OPTICAL-SCAN VOTE-COUNTING SYSTEM

The optical-scan system uses paper ballots and a dark leaded pencil. Voters either fill in circles to indicate their choices or complete a line connecting the head and tail of an arrow that points to their choice.

THE 2000 ELECTION

In the 2000 presidential race between Republican George W. Bush and Democrat Albert Gore, the first count indicated that Bush had won Florida by 1,784 votes. According to Florida law, election results showing a difference of one-tenth of 1 percent or less automatically triggers a statewide recount. This recount is conducted in the same manner as the first count. The second recount indicated that Bush's lead had dropped to 327 votes, with the absentee ballots yet to be counted. Exercising the right of the losing candidate, Gore requested a hand count in four counties: Miami-Dade, Broward, Palm Beach, and Volusia. Although the difference narrowed at times, Bush held the lead throughout the recounts. Questions arose about the intent of the voters on whose ballots the chads were not removed, were only slightly indented, or showed evidence of a vote for more than one candidate. No one had experience in this situation, and Florida had no standard for judging the intent of the voter in hand counting the punch-card ballots. The Republicans filed suit as the standards changed, and the count was finally ended by the U.S. Supreme Court on December 12, 2000, more than a month after the November 7 election. When the counting stopped, Florida secretary of state Katherine Harris certified the vote with Bush's lead at 537 votes. George W. Bush won Florida's 25 electoral votes and became the 43rd president of the United States.

After the voter marks all of his or her choices, he or she can review the ballot. If all the choices are correct, the voter then feeds the ballot into the optical-scan vote-counting machine. The scanner reads the pencil-darkened areas on the ballot, counts the votes, and stores the paper ballot in a secure compartment (ballot box). Should questions arise about the accuracy of the count, the paper ballots can be counted again. This can be done by repeating the machine count or counting the ballots by hand. With the optical scan, the electronic count is fast and offers a quick tally on a removable disk plus the benefit of a paper ballot. Most people find this voting method easy, and they are comfortable with the security of this system.

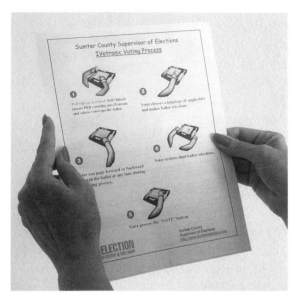

Instructions for using voting systems are provided by each county. This voter is sharing instructions for voting on the iVotronic voting system introduced in Florida in 2002. *(Photo by author)*

DIRECT RECORDING ELECTRONIC VOTING SYSTEMS

Another method of vote counting is the direct recording electronic (DRE) voting machine. These machines use current computer technology. Some DREs show the ballot on a monitor screen and allow the voter to make choices by scrolling, highlighting, and clicking, much as one views a Web page using a mouse. Others such as iVotronic, display the ballot on a touch-sensitive screen. The voter makes selections by touching the screen. In both types of DRE machines, the voter can check his or her choices before casting a vote. The vote is instantly counted and recorded electronically on the equivalent of a computer hard drive and a removable disk. Some electronic machines, however, do not print paper ballots, and in the case of a recount, the result on the hard drive and removable disk do not prove how the voters voted. They only offer a copy of the information that was recorded on the disk. Some people have faith in the accuracy of these computers. Others, however, fear that tampering is possible and demand that all machines have the ability to print a paper ballot that the voter can see and deposit in a ballot box to accompany the information on the hard drive and removable disk.

In 2004, California and other states began taking steps to require that DRE voting machines provide a verifiable paper trail.

No matter which machines are used, official election results take time to compile. News organizations do not wait for the official outcome of an election. They use their own methods to project (predict) the winners.

"There's no way to run a reliable election without a verifiable paper trail—that's what these machines don't have."

—David Dill, Stanford University computer science professor, November 2003

EXIT POLLS AND NETWORK PROJECTIONS

Election Day is exciting, and just about everyone wants to know the outcome as soon as possible.

In the early days of television, beginning with the 1952 election, CBS used a massive computer called Univac to project the winners. The computer took the final precinct numbers from past elections and the incomplete count in the current election and mathematically projected the likely final count. This method proved to be accurate. However, the projection could not begin until the polls closed and the precincts began reporting.

In about 1980, the news organizations began relying on information gained in exit polls for their projections. Exit pollsters question voters as they leave the polls to find out how they voted and why. Based on this information, news organizations would sometimes predict the winner of an election long before the polls close.

Early projections and the different time zones complicate the national election process. When polls close at 8:00 P.M. on the East Coast, it is only 5:00 P.M. on the West Coast and polls will be open for another three hours. In addition, a presidential candidate can win more than the 270 electoral votes (and the election) in eastern and central states long before the polls close in the western states.

Consequently, the early announcement of a presidential winner can affect state and local elections in the West as well as the presidential popular vote. Once the winner is announced, people who have not yet voted may be discouraged and think their vote will not count, so many of them may not vote. For example, in the 1980 presidential election, the networks announced Ronald Reagan's victory over Jimmy Carter based on early exit poll projections in the East. Furthermore, Jimmy Carter's concession speech was televised two hours before the polls closed on West Coast. In 2003, Thomas E. Patterson, a professor at Harvard University, completed a research project on election night broadcasts. He wrote in his report, issued by the university's John F. Kennedy School of Government, that "[t]he 1980 presidential election is the one instance where West Coast turnout clearly sagged after the networks named a winner." After that election (thought to alter the outcome of state and local elections) Congress considered legislation that would eliminate this problem. Some debate was given to passing a law that would set a uniform time (based on one time zone) for closing all polls on Election Day. This approach, however, is unacceptable because it interferes with the states' authority to conduct elections. Congress also considered passing a law that would prohibit

"It goes without saying that once the polling places are closed, the winner has been chosen. But we don't know who it is! Nor can we know until boxes are opened, ballots counted and the results announced. That takes too long and is much too dull."

—*Reuven Frank, NBC network journalist who was a pioneer in TV election coverage*

announcing the projected presidential winner until all polls across the nation had closed. This approach interferes with freedom of the press guaranteed in the Constitution.

While Congress debated, the networks agreed among themselves that they would not announce the winner until most of the polls had closed in each state. They made this promise to Congress in 1985.

The issue surfaced again in the 2000 presidential election. Several networks announced the Florida exit poll projection before the

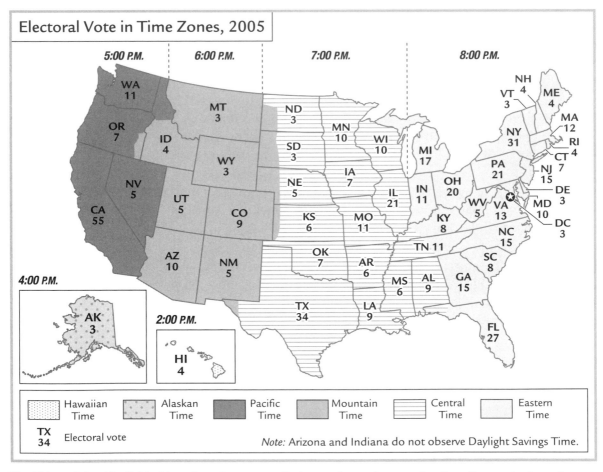

The U.S. mainland is divided into four time zones. Each zone is one hour earlier than the one to its east. This means that East Coast polls close three hours earlier than West Coast polls. As a result, a presidential candidate can acquire enough electoral votes in the eastern states to win an election long before polls close in the western half of the United States.

polls had closed throughout the state. Two time zones slice through Florida. Although the polls closed at 8:00 P.M. in the portion of the state in the Eastern time zone, in Florida's panhandle (in the Central time zone), it was only 7:00 P.M. Panhandle polls would not close for another hour. Although NBC, CBS, CNN, Fox, ABC, and the Associated Press called Florida for Albert Gore, the race was actually too close to call. A few hours later, Bush's count moved into a narrow lead. From that point on, the Florida presidential election made history that brought about many changes in the U.S. election process, including the passage of HAVA.

In 2004, Democratic candidates John Kerry and John Edwards challenged the Republican incumbents, George W. Bush and Dick Cheney. By early afternoon on November 2 (Election Day), some Web sites had announced early exit poll results indicating that Kerry had a lead over Bush in the swing states (states that were thought likely to determine the outcome of the 2004 election but where the vote was too close to predict in preelection tracking polls). Early voters, however, do not represent a wide enough range of voters to accurately predict the outcome of an election. Consequently, this information was misleading. Still, Kerry supporters were encouraged and Bush supporters were discouraged. Later in the day, the trend changed to indicate a Bush lead that continued to the final tally.

Network viewers want to know the outcome of an election as much as each news organization wants to be the first to reveal it. The news organizations argue that they have a constitutional right and the responsibility to deliver news as soon as they know it. However, many people believe that announcing early projections influences the vote in western states. News organizations are businesses that compete for viewers. They are not officials who have taken an oath to participate in a fair and honest election.

9

Threats to Democracy
and Freedom

"In a republic the first rule for the guidance of the citizen is obedience to the law. . . . The essence of a republic is representative government. Our Congress represents the people and the States. In all legislative affairs it is the natural collaborator [partner] with the President."

—*President Calvin Coolidge, Inaugural Address, March 4, 1925*

For most Americans, the word *democracy* brings to mind freedom, the American way of government, and the right to vote. People believe that freedom is an American heritage. Exercising the right to vote helps protect this treasure. Many people, however, mistakenly think that the United States is a democracy. It is a republic.

DEMOCRACY VS. REPUBLIC

A democracy and a republic are different forms of government. In a pure democracy, the majority rules. The voters decide everything. For example, after an attack on a country with a pure democratic government, the people would vote on how and when to defend the country. Many or most of them might have little knowledge of the country's power or the attacker's strength. By the time a vote could be held, an attacker might have the country under siege and the people in bondage. Ancient Greece was a democracy. A republic, however, is a government based on law (a constitution). The eligible voters elect officials to represent them in making governmental decisions under this law. The elected officials take an oath to support and defend the law, which in the United States is the Constitution. They are expected to be knowledgeable and make decisions for the common good of the people.

The founders of the U.S. Republic purposely placed governmental decisions in the hands of elected representatives. They believed that most voters would not have the knowledge needed to make major, complicated decisions and could be influenced by foreign powers. They also believed that the people (voters) could be unduly influenced by political activists who placed the political party's desire for power above the common good of the nation.

PARTISAN POLITICS

When George Washington retired from office, he wrote in his farewell speech that the spirit of the party

> serves always to distract the Public Councils, and enfeeble the Public Administration. It agitates the Community with ill-founded jealousies and false alarms; kindles the animosity of one part against another, foments [incites] occasionally riot and insurrection. It opens the door to foreign influence and corruption, which find a facilitated [easy] access to the government itself through the channels of party passions.

Most of George Washington's warnings have proved true. Win-at-all-cost campaign strategies often include an attempt to deceive the voters by discrediting one candidate with distortion and false implications while glorifying and exaggerating the qualities of the other. Unfortunately, there is no legal penalty for lying during a political campaign. The voters are left to seek the truth for themselves. Truth-finding is made difficult by political campaigns that use deceptive tactics to influence voters. Politicians know that what the voters believe (not necessarily the truth) on Election Day determines the outcome of the election.

Another major threat of partisan politics comes from elected officials who do not have the courage to vote their conscience (what they believe to be right). Elected on promises and partisan policies, many seem to forget that they are representatives of, not one party, but all the people living in the region they represent. They represent these people in deciding what is good for the nation. It is their duty to study the issues and evaluate the possible consequences of all options. Their legislative vote should reflect their honest opinion of what is best for the nation. John F. Kennedy wrote in his book *Profiles in Courage* that "when party and office holder differ as to how the national interest is to be served, we must place the first responsibility we owe not to our party or even to our constituents, but to our individual consciences."

Voters, too, have a responsibility to consider the national interest, or common good, in making their choices. They have a duty to evaluate the candidate's current stand on the issues, reputation, and political record. Gaining the information necessary to make an educated choice is not easy when the candidates conduct win-at-all-cost campaigns.

POLITICAL MACHINES

In the late 1800s and early 1900s, the major parties created "political machines" to win elections and take control of large city governments. Professional politicians became the "bosses" of these political machines. The political machine gained power by exchanging jobs for votes. Politicians often went into poor neighborhoods where many immigrants lived. They helped these people with the naturalization process and basic needs such as employment and housing.

These politicians then pressured people to vote a certain way. In addition, ward captains (local party leaders) made sure the voters turned out. If needed, thugs paid a visit and used strong-arm tactics to persuade the voter to go to the polls.

These intimidated people lost the power of their vote to the political machine. The bosses and their cronies took over city government through the corrupted election process. Once in office, they overcharged for city improvements and funneled large amounts of public money into their own hands. Historians estimate that one political boss, William M. "Boss" Tweed, swindled as much as $200 million from New York City. In 1871, with the city near bankruptcy, Tweed was arrested and charged with several counts of corruption. He was convicted and sentenced to 12 years in prison plus a $12,750 fine.

The corruption of New York City politics is an example of the devastation that can result when voters are intimidated by strong-arm methods. Other methods of stealing the power of the vote are less forceful but still a threat to democracy and the Republic.

"What tells in holding your grip on your district is to go right down among the poor families and help them. I've got a regular system for this. If there's a fire . . . I'm usually there with some of my election district captains as soon as the fire engines. If a family is burned out . . . I get quarters [housing] for them, buy clothes for them . . . and fix them up until they get things runnin' again. It's philanthropy (charity), but it's politics too—mighty good politics. Who can tell me how many votes one of those fires brings me? The poor are the most grateful people in the world, and, let me tell you, they have more friends in their neighborhoods than the rich have in theirs . . ."

—*George Washington Plunkitt, politician,
New York, 1889*

This 1871 political cartoon shows Boss Tweed as a bullying teacher giving New York City comptroller Richard B. Connolly a lesson in wildly inaccurate arithmetic. *(Library of Congress, Prints and Photographs Division [LC-USZ62-8875])*

VOTER FRAUD

Voter fraud is an organized effort to elect a candidate by using trickery, deceit, or deception in voter registration or casting ballots. Reports of vote fraud clouded the political scene soon after the formation of political parties in the early 1800s. One of the first documented accounts occurred in New York City in 1844. The city had about 41,000 eligible voters. However, 55,000 votes were cast at the polls.

In more recent years, voter fraud has involved absentee ballots. For example, in 1993 Democrat Bill Stinson lost at the polls in Philadelphia's Second District state senate race. The unusually high number of 1,757 absentee ballots, however, changed the outcome

MYSTERIOUS BALLOT BOX 13

In 1948, Texas congressman Lyndon Baines Johnson and Texas governor Coke Stevenson competed in the Democratic primary for the U.S. Senate nomination. When the polls closed on Election Day, the count was close, with Stevenson ahead by a narrow margin. Then the returns came in from Alice, Texas. Ballot Box 13 moved Lyndon Johnson into the lead by 87 votes. The next January, Johnson was sworn in as a senator from Texas. This launched him on a political journey that would lead to the White House in 1963. The suspicious contents of Ballot Box 13 raised questions about the honesty of the election. According to the *Dallas Morning News,* the box contained 201 votes for Johnson and two for Stevenson. Polling place records showed that the votes had been cast in alphabetical order and marked with the same pen. To make matters more suspicious, many people listed as having voted were out of town on Election Day, were not registered, or were dead. The candidates belonged to the same party, and both were thought to have collected a few questionable votes. Consequently, no charges were filed.

Lyndon B. Johnson served as Senate majority leader and vice president of the United States before becoming president upon President John F. Kennedy's death. *(Library of Congress, U.S. News & World Report Magazine Photograph Collection [LC-U91-242-2])*

of the election and gave Stinson the victory. Suspecting fraud, a news organization began an investigation. The *Philadelphia Inquirer* compared signatures on the absentee ballots, voter registration cards, and poll books. This part of the investigation revealed that many people had voted an absentee ballot and voted again at the polls in person. The newspaper also created computer databases with information gleaned from voter registration cards and county records. Database searches determined that many ballots had been cast in the names of people who no longer lived in the district. (Some had moved and others had died.) In interviews with voters, reporters found that Stinson supporters had campaigned in the barrios (Latin American neighborhoods) of North Philadelphia during the last weeks of the campaign. They had pressured people to vote for Stinson by absentee ballot and sometimes marked the ballots to be sure they did as they were told.

Campaign activists often target a group of people who are eligible to register but unlikely to vote, such as the homeless, residents of public housing, newly naturalized immigrants, and elderly people living in nursing homes. Many of these people have little interest in politics and limited knowledge about the candidates or ballot questions. They do have needs, however, and welcome promises of government programs that will improve their lives. Consequently, they are easily influenced by paid workers conducting get-out-the-vote registration and absentee ballot drives.

VOTER APATHY

Some people find politics boring. They do not care about issues, and they do not vote. They mistakenly think that the outcome of an election will not affect them. Voter apathy (lack of interest) is one of the biggest threats to democracy. Citizens who do not vote actually give more power to those who do. Whatever the citizen's view, not voting gives more power to voters with opposing viewpoints.

Citizens with an apathetic attitude and no concern for the election process offer a field of voters ripe for the harvest. The lure of a large number of unregistered voters prompts the major parties to conduct get-out-the vote drives. In addition, the combination of easy registration and easy voting has resulted in more opportunities for fraud.

MOTOR VOTER LAW AND "NO FAULT" ABSENTEE BALLOTS

Hans A. von Spackovsky, an attorney and government affairs consultant, testified before a Senate committee on May 9, 2001, that when the 1993 Motor Voter Act is "combined with absentee voting, an individual can register and cast an absentee ballot without any

> "The ballot is the most powerful nonviolent tool we have in a democracy. And if that is threatened, we won't have much left."
>
> —*Representative John Lewis (Democrat–Georgia) quoted in the* Atlanta Journal-Constitution, *February 15, 2004*

election official ever seeing him. This makes multiple registrations and multiple votes very easy."

Arizona, Colorado, Oregon, and California were among the first states to allow any registered voter to request an absentee ballot without stating a reason. By 2000, 23 states had passed "no fault" absentee ballot laws. Several other states followed after the 2000 election, including Florida, Indiana, and North Carolina. In states that relaxed regulations on absentee ballots, political parties increase their get-out-the-vote operations in the last weeks before an election. According to Spackovsky, "No fault absentee ballot laws make it easier for campaign organizations to engage in tactics such as requesting absentee ballots in the names of low-income housing residents and senior citizens and either intimidating them into casting votes or completing their ballots for them." Residents of nursing homes are also prime targets.

Absentee ballots make vote buying easier by eliminating the security of the secret ballot and privacy of the voting booth. The vote buyer can oversee the vote and mail the ballot. This makes vote buying a cash-and-carry business.

Since 1993, reports of voter fraud involving absentee ballots and registration cards have increased. For example, on October 31, 2002, the *Washington Times* reported that an Arkansas campaign staffer had hired two teenagers to register voters. The usual procedure is that paid workers receive a dollar or two for each registration. In this case, the teens increased their earnings by filling out hundreds of registration cards with names and addresses they found in the phone book. The names included businesses and dead people. While many cases are not prosecuted, serious violators are tried, convicted, and sentenced, such as the one reported in the Covington *Kentucky Post,* March 17, 2004. According to the report, Donnie Newsome, the highest elected official in Knott County, Tennessee, was convicted of two counts of buying votes and one count of conspiracy to buy votes in the 1998 primary election. His sentence included two years and two months in prison, three years' probation, and a $20,000 fine.

MEDIA INFLUENCE

Much of the American public depends on news organizations for information concerning the candidates' stand on issues and fitness for office. However, the media reports the news as seen through the reporters' eyes, and, some people believe, as influenced by corporations that own the TV networks and newspapers.

Consequently, news stories are often biased. Many people complain about the biased media. Liberals (mostly Democrats) complain about what they see as a conservative bias on editorial pages and in radio and TV talk show hosts. Conservatives (mostly Republicans) complain that a majority of news reporters hold liberal views. Some people complain that the news is more geared to selling papers or attracting viewers than to informing the public.

In reality, most editorial writers and talk radio and TV hosts are openly biased. In addition, most news reports are biased although much of this bias is unintentional. It happens naturally. Every report is influenced by the attitudes and background of the people who prepare the presentation (writer, editor, photographer, and so on) and by the audience it serves. This can become a threat to the Republic when voters allow just one news source to dictate their

> "Any work of journalism is saturated with bias from the moment the reporter leaves the office . . . to the edited and finished product. I see it everywhere. I often disagree with those who see it only *somewhere* in the press . . ."
>
> —*Jay Rosen, press critic and professor of journalism at New York University, May 22, 2004*

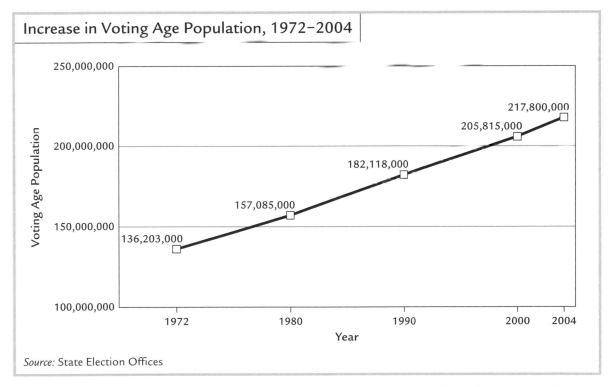

Increase in Voting Age Population, 1972–2004

Source: State Election Offices

Conducting an election has become a more difficult task as the voting age population has increased. This graph shows the increase between 1972 and 2004. The figures are based on the U.S. census and include many people who are not eligible to vote.

election choices or when there is nowhere to find complete, accurate information. These voters may not have enough information to choose the candidate who best supports their views on the issues. The press is a valuable tool for informing voters, but it also has the power to deceive.

Media fraud (a far more dangerous issue than bias) occurs if members of the media influence voters by deliberately distorting the facts in reporting current events, campaign activities, or a candidate's message. Thomas Sowell, Hoover Institute Fellow at Stanford University, wrote that "In a country where the masses choose their leaders and influence policies, a fraudulent press can mislead the voters into national disaster." The U.S. Constitution, however, gives the press almost unchallengeable freedom of speech. Therefore, the public can best protect itself by seeking information from several sources and knowing the bias of these sources.

There are many threats to American freedom. This has been true for more than 200 years. As the right to vote has been extended, voter turnout increased to more than 100 million in 1984, and the voting age population reached almost 206 million in 2000. Congress has taken steps to protect this right with legislation and amendments to the Constitution. Much of the responsibility, however, falls to the individual voters, candidates running for office, and members of the press.

10

Valuing the Right to Vote

By the time the United States celebrated its 200th birthday, eight amendments had been added to U.S. Constitution to expand the electorate. In the process, every law-abiding, mentally competent adult citizen gained the right to vote. During this time, Congress passed other legislation designed to protect the right to vote and encourage voter turnout. The right to vote, however, can be lost or lose its value if not protected by its owner, the individual citizen.

The best way citizens can protect this right (and all others) is by voting.

> "Democracy is a promise, not a guarantee."
>
> —Joan Paik, League of Women Voters chair of election administration reform, May 22, 2001

DECLINE IN VOTER TURNOUT

Voter turnout has declined since 1960. When the electorate is divided by age, voters 65 and older have the highest voter turnout and the 18-to-20-year-olds have the lowest. Several organizations, including Rock the Vote, New Voters Project, Citizen Change, and Declare Yourself, worked to register new young voters before the 2004 presidential election. This effort increased the young voter turnout. However, all voters turned out in record numbers in 2004. Consequently, the percent of the total vote represented by 18–24-year-old voters in 2004 was approximately 10 percent, about the same as for the 2000 election.

Experts believe that people who do not begin voting when they come of age are less likely to vote when they grow older. Consequently, young voters' lack of interest and participation in the election process is of major concern. Many groups are working to

> "Elections belong to the people. It is their decision. If they decide to turn their back on the fire and burn their behinds, then they will just have to sit on their blisters."
>
> —*Abraham Lincoln (1809–1865)*

reverse this trend. In order to convince young people to get involved, it helps to try and understand why many are not interested.

Several studies have been conducted to find out why people (especially the young) do not vote. The evidence is fairly clear that many do not care about politics or are disillusioned by it. These same people think that their one vote does not make a difference or that the outcome of an election does not affect them in their daily life. Many education organizations, such as the Center for Governmental Studies at the University of Virginia and the National Center for Education, believe that these attitudes reflect the decrease in civics education over the past few decades. Many other young voters may feel that none of the candidates appeal to them and/or that the system itself is flawed.

Educated Voters

Civics and government classes educate students about the organization of the U.S. government, the responsibilities of the judicial, legislative, and executive branches and how they work together and hold each other accountable, plus the election process and responsibilities of good citizenship. Civics and government classes began to slip from the school curriculum at about the same time that American history, civics, government, and multicultural studies were combined into social studies. This merger reduced the amount of class time available for studying government and civics.

> "Politics ought to be the part-time profession of every citizen who would protect the rights and privileges of free people and who would preserve what is good and fruitful in our national heritage."
>
> —*Dwight D. Eisenhower, July 12, 1945*

When today's senior citizens attended grade school, the day began with the flag salute, as did every assembly, ball game, and graduation ceremony. Grade-school American history included the founding of the nation, with time spent learning about the U.S. government. (Good citizenship was expected.) When these students reached junior high and high school, a semester of civics partnered with a semester of state history awaited them. Social studies and multicultural studies were yet to be invented. Older members of this age group fought in World War II. Some of its younger men went to Korea. They were raised in such a way that most accepted voting as a civic duty that must be carried out without question. Most of these people vote.

Their voting record did not pass to the younger generations. U.S. Senator Zell Miller (Democrat–Georgia), a member of this generation, explained his opinion of this failure in his book *A*

National Party No More: "Loving and well-meaning parents are so intent on giving their children what they didn't have when they were growing up that they have failed to give them what they did have: a sense of place, a sense of family, a code of conduct, a set of values."

Other people would argue that perhaps the decline seen in voter turnout mirrored the country's disillusionment with governments and presidents beginning with U.S. involvement in Vietnam during the Johnson years and heightened after the Watergate scandal, involving President Richard Nixon. Young people of the generations born following World War II were raised in an atmosphere where questioning authority and the way things had been done was viewed as the way to improve society. To them, dissent could be patriotic.

Whatever the cause, student knowledge has declined. In 1998, about 22,000 students in grades four, eight, and 12 took the National Center for Education Statistics (NCES) civics test. Only 26 percent of those in grade 12 scored at "proficient" level or above. This means that about 74 percent of high school graduates did not have a clear understanding of how the U.S. government works and what responsibilities one has as a citizen. At that time, only 29 states required courses in government or civics for graduating high school. Dakota Draper, an eighth-grade history teacher in North Dakota, sees a clear link between civics education and protecting democracy: "If our kids walk out of our school systems without an understanding of democracy, democracy will cease." Many educators at all levels are concerned that too little time is spent teaching students U.S. history and the qualities of responsible citizenship. Of course, civics and U.S. government are not the only subjects in which educators are concerned by students' decline in knowledge and test scores. Improvement of the overall U.S. education system might also help raise civics proficiency.

In 2003, the National Conference of State Legislatures prepared a report titled *Citizenship* based on interviews of young citizens under age 26. This report concluded that only two-thirds of America's young people believe that voting is a good-citizenship requirement. The report also compared those who had taken a civics class with those who had not. Seventy-two percent of voting age participants who took civics classes registered to vote, and 59 percent

> "All who have mediated in the art of governing mankind have been convinced that the fate of empires depends on the education of youth."
>
> —*Aristotle*
> *(384–322 B.C.)*

actually voted. Among those who said they did not take a civics class, 43 percent registered and only 28 percent voted. This report indicates that civic education increases voter registration and turnout.

Civics education might also include educating young people about their government and civic responsibilities plus helping them to understand what the campaign issues mean to their future and the candidates' views of these issues.

Informed Voters

After the November 2, 2004, election, Hans Reimer, political director for Rock the Vote, said that young people voted because the effort to register young voters "convinced the parties and media to focus on them." Like other voters, young people received the information they needed when candidates addressed the issues that are important to them. These informed young people voted because, according to Reimer, "They felt like the issues made a big difference in their lives. They felt like it really mattered." Gaining accurate information about the candidates' backgrounds, experience, stand on the issues, and plan of action if they are elected, however, is not easy because of the media's tendency to treat civic matters as entertainment.

In most campaigns, personal attacks and conflicts between candidates are given more attention than policy speeches in an effort to heighten tension and create the sense of thrill that comes from a competition. Cokie Roberts, a reporter for ABC television and National Public Radio, wrote in an article for the Center for Media Literacy that the large number of "[j]ournalists covering any campaign will hear and report the same speech endlessly. The good ones run issue pieces as well. But people tend to pay the most attention to personality stories [and] character confrontations." In attempts to gain public attention for their news organizations, reporters search for the most exciting phrases in a candidate's speech. These sound bites are often negative remarks about the opponent rather than positive statements concerning the issues. Consequently, the public is exposed to far more negative than positive information about each candidate. When the time comes to make a decision, voters are more likely to know whom they are against than whom they are for. Filled with negative information about the candidates and feeling that there are no good choices, the voter may not vote.

Accurate information is often available, and citizens can make themselves informed voters. It, however, takes some effort.

Most candidates have Web sites where they list their biographical experience, political record, and issue statements. Several organizations, including the League of Women Voters and Project Vote Smart, make similar information available on their Web sites. The League of Women Voters, which grew out of the women's suffrage movement, has always been politically active. They take a position on issues that are important to women and identify candidates who support their view of these issues. In addition, the League of Women Voters promotes voter education and hosts candidate debates. There are other organizations that also take an interest in issues that are important to their followers and whose Web sites provide information. Just as with the other news media, one must know and take into consideration the bias of a Web site. Project Vote Smart is an information-only organization that takes no position on the issues.

> "Knowledge will forever govern ignorance; and a people who mean to be their own governors must arm themselves with the power which knowledge gives."
>
> —*James Madison, member of the Constitutional Convention and fourth president of the United States, 1822*

CONCERNED VOTERS

In a time of uncertain economic change, with the United States fighting overseas and worried about terrorism at home, young people have many concerns for the future. By exercising their right to vote, young citizens can have a say in how that future is shaped.

Some organizations working to register young people to vote and help them value and use that right are trying to make a connection between concerns of the young and politics. These organizations include Rock the Vote, New Voters Project, Citizen Change, and Declare Yourself.

In a September 15, 2004, article, the *New York Times* told of 22-year-old Marie Reyes, who did not vote in the 2000 election, because, she said, "Nothing in that election ever remotely related to my life." But in the months before the 2004 election, Reyes was busy volunteering to register voters in her state, New Mexico, knowing that in the 2000 election, that state was decided by only 366 votes. She now understood that every vote matters.

If young citizens come to feel that their votes do matter and that they can have an impact by supporting candidates who share

PROJECT VOTE SMART

In 1986, after Democrat Richard Kimble lost to Republican John McCain in the Arizona Senate race, Kimble's campaign staff began tossing around ideas to improve the political process. They thought that most campaigns offered a lot of confusing hype with little of the accurate political information that voters need to make their ballot decisions.

By 1990, this small group had a plan to provide voters with accurate, nonpartisan information about the candidates. They set up a toll-free hotline and began answering voters' questions. By 1992, the organization had attracted the interest of 40 national political leaders, both liberals and conservatives. The impressive list included former senators Barry Goldwater (Republican–Arizona) and George McGovern (Democrat–South Dakota); Representative Newt Gingrich (Republican–Georgia); and former representative Geraldine Ferraro (Democrat–New York). In addition, former presidents Gerald Ford (Republican) and Jimmy Carter (Democrat) served as honorary cofounders.

In the mid-1990s, Project Vote Smart took advantage of the expanding Internet and created a Web site (http://www.vote-smart.org) offering voters information on candidates' positions plus their voting records and experience. As evidence that many voters do want to be informed, during the 2000 presidential primaries the site claimed to average more than 1 million hits a day.

their concerns, many people believe, more young people will vote. Based on state and national exit polls, 10–12 million people ages 18–24 voted in the 2004 presidential election. This means that 42–47 percent of eligible voters in this age group voted in 2004, compared to 36.5 percent in 2000.

ROCK THE VOTE

In 1990, members of the recording industry formed a nonprofit, nonpartisan group called Rock the Vote. Their mission, as stated on their Web site (http://www.rockthevote.com) is "protecting freedom of expression and empowering young people to change their world." People from the entertainment community work with the organization to attract the attention of young people.

In 1991, Rock the Vote supported the National Voter Registration Reform Act (NVRA), also known as the Motor Voter Bill, and waged a write-in campaign to Congress, which passed the bill (later vetoed by President George H. W. Bush but then signed by President Bill Clinton). The group has produced public service announcements and television specials featuring such celebrities as Queen Latifah, Aerosmith, Madonna, and Whoopi Goldberg. Many of the celebrities who participate in these events are known to have strong liberal views. According to Rock the Vote's Web site, activities such as these helped lead more than 2 million new young voters to the polls in 1992. Rock the Vote continued its work through the elections of 1996, 2000, and 2004. A visit to the Web site allows users to see voting information, read a blog that reports news of the interest to young people, volunteer, and—most important—register to vote.

Most voters do not have time to make themselves aware of everything all candidates have said and done. However, each person has some issues they consider most important. Issue statements and voting records are indexed on these sites, allowing voters to compare the candidates' views on issues that are most important to them.

After informed voters have gained the information to make their decisions, Election Day awaits. To make their decisions count, however, they need to know where, when, and how to vote.

VOTER RESPONSIBILITY

Some people think voting is complicated and feel intimidated by the voting process. Information to ease these concerns can be easily obtained by calling the state or county election office or visiting the Federal Election Commission Web page.

Some states mail sample ballots to all registered voters a few weeks before every election. In some counties, the sample ballot is addressed to each registered voter. In others, it is addressed to "the registered voters at" the address. The sample ballot usually includes information on each ballot question, an example of the complete ballot, and illustrated instructions on marking the ballot. The polling place is usually indicated on the outside of the sample ballot booklet near the voter's address.

The voter's polling place is determined by that person's address. Therefore, the post office does not forward sample ballots. Voters who move are required to notify the county election officials of their new address. If the move is outside the county, a new registration is required. Voters are allowed to vote only at their designated polling place, where their registration information appears on the voter rolls.

Voters must follow the instructions to be sure their vote will count. For example, most paper ballots must be marked with a number-two pencil so that they can be read by the optical-scan vote-counting machine. Marks on the ballot other than those indicating the voter's choice may mean that the machine cannot read the ballot. A botched ballot should be exchanged for a new one.

In each presidential election from 1988 to 2000, about 1.7 million of approximately 100 million ballots cast were rejected by the vote-counting machines. The count in most states in most elections is not close enough for the number of rejected ballots in that state to change the outcome of an election. Florida 2000 was an

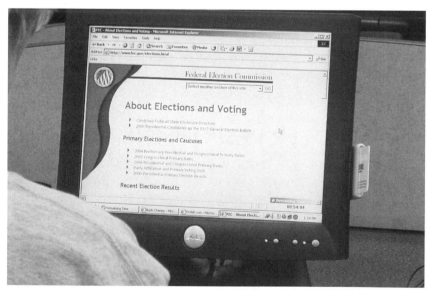

This voter is using a computer at her local library. A peek over her shoulder reveals some of the links to information on the Federal Election Commission's Web site. *(Photo by author)*

A voter carefully marks her choice using a number two pencil as instructed on the ballot. *(Photo by author)*

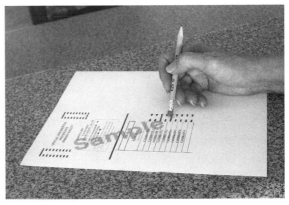

This voter has made an error. The erasure will leave a smudge. To be certain the vote will count, she should request a replacement ballot. *(Photo by author)*

exception. Most of the rejected ballots would have been counted if the voters had followed the instructions clearly printed on the ballot and the sample ballot.

The right to vote is every U.S. citizen's precious possession. It was purchased with the blood of past generations and is preserved by the valor of every generation. This treasure is a birthright, held in trust for each American child until he or she comes of age. It comes with responsibility and must be claimed by meeting state requirements and registering. Its use ensures all qualified citizens a voice in the government and protects all other rights.

Glossary

abolitionists   People who wanted to end the practice of slavery.

antifederalists   Writers of the U.S. Constitution and early leaders who opposed a strong federal (centralized) government and favored leaving more governmental power to the states.

Australian ballot   The secret-ballot form of voting invented in Australia and first used in the United States in the early 1800s.

bias   Favoring one side or opinion over another, such as a political leaning in a news report.

bill   Legislation considered or passed by a legislative body. A bill that is passed becomes law.

campaign strategy   The plan a political campaign organization creates in its effort to win election.

canvass   To count the votes after voters have cast their ballots.

civics   The study of citizens' rights and responsibilities.

Confederacy   Southern states that seceded from the Union in 1861 and united into a separate nation, also known as the Confederate States of America.

conservative   The political viewpoint that favors smaller federal government with more power in state government and individual responsibility.

constituents   The people whom an elected official represents.

democracy   A form of government in which the people vote on every issue and the majority rules; a true democracy has no elected representatives.

Democratic-Republican   One of the first political parties that had formed by the end of George Washington's second term as U.S. president.

discriminatory   Refusing some people rights or privileges that are given to others.

disenfranchise   To take away someone's right to vote.

electorate   Officially qualified voters.

enfranchise   Give someone the right to vote.

federalists   Writers of the U.S. Constitution and early leaders who favored a strong federal government.

felony   A serious crime with a severe penalty.

franchise   The right to vote.

indentured   Bound by an agreement to work several years to repay the fare for passage to America, usually from Great Britain.

institution   An established organization, law, custom, or practice.

intimidation   The use of bullying, violence, or fear to make someone do something.

liberal   A person who believes in a strong federal government and the protection of personal freedom.

mentally incompetent   Unable to make decisions for oneself.

misdemeanor   A minor crime with mild punishment.

nonpartisan   Favoring no political party.

opinion polls   Questionnaires and surveys presented to a group of people to discover their views on certain matters, often political.

opponent   A person in opposition to another, such as another candidate.

partisan   Acting in accordance with a political party's agenda or its basic beliefs.

party-line voters   People who always vote for the candidates of their political party.

precinct   The area in which residents are eligible to vote at a particular polling place.

pollsters   People hired to ask the public questions and gather information for a poll.

ratify   To give formal approval, as when the states approve a constitutional amendment.

republic   A nation with a representative form of government based on law, such as the U.S. government based on the U.S. Constitution.

representative government   A form of government in which the people elect representatives to make governmental decisions.

suffrage   The right to vote.

suffragist   Political activist in the 1800s and early 1900s who worked to gain the right to vote for African Americans and women.

swing voters   People who are likely to vote for the candidates of either major party.

vigilante   A person who takes the law into his or her own hands without proper legal proceedings.

Chronology

1763–75

◆ After the French and Indian War ends in 1763, the British levy a series of taxes on the American colonies beginning with the Sugar Act in 1764 and ending with the Coercive Acts passed in 1774–75 in response to the Boston Tea Party.

1775–81

◆ During the Revolutionary War, which began at Lexington, Massachusetts, and ended at Yorktown, Virginia, the American colonies win the right to representation (the vote) in the legislative body that governs them.

1787

◆ The Constitutional Convention creates the Constitution, establishing the government of the United States. The Constitution guarantees a government by the people but leaves how and who would vote up to the individual states. At this time, voting requirements in most states are based on English common law—only adult white male property owners have the right to vote. The New Jersey state constitution allows women the vote.

1788

◆ *June 21:* New Hampshire becomes the ninth state to ratify the Constitution, and the U.S. Constitution becomes the law of the land.

1789

◆ In an electoral process that follows the requirements of the Constitution, George Washington is elected president of the United States. He receives all 69 electoral votes.

1804

◆ *June 15:* The Twelfth Amendment changes presidential election guidelines so that the president and vice president are elected on separate ballots.

1807

◆ Women lose the right to vote in New Jersey. Women will not gain the universal right to vote in the United States for more than a century.

1830s

◆ Women, including the Grimké sisters, become politically active in the antislavery movement.

1848

◆ *July 19–20:* The first women's suffrage convention is held in Seneca Falls, New York. The signing of the Declaration of Sentiments ends the convention and marks the official beginning of the women's suffrage movement.

1857

◆ *March 6:* In the *Dred Scott* decision, the Supreme Court rules that a slave of African descent cannot be a U.S. citizen. The Court also rules the Missouri Compromise unconstitutional. This court decision brought the United States to the brink of civil war.

1860

◆ *December 20:* South Carolina becomes the first southern state to secede from the Union over disagreements with the federal government over slavery and free trade. Other southern states soon join South Carolina in forming the Confederacy.

1861

◆ *April 12:* Confederate troops fire on Fort Sumter and the Civil War begins.

1865

◆ *December 6:* After the Civil War ends, the Thirteenth Amendment abolishes slavery.

1868

◆ *July 9:* The Fourteenth Amendment grants citizenship to all persons born in the United States (including former slaves). Section 2 of this amendment uses the word *male* to identify voters and constitutionally denies women the right to vote.

1869

◆ A second suffrage organization, the National American Woman Suffrage Association, forms with Susan B. Anthony serving as president.

1870

◆ *February 17:* The Fifteenth Amendment prohibits state and local governments from denying men the right to vote based on race, color, or having been a slave. This establishes black men's right to vote.

1872

◆ *November 5:* Susan B. Anthony casts a ballot in a federal election although women do not have the right to vote. This practice is commonly used by suffragists who hope to file suit and win the right to vote in court.
◆ *November 18:* Susan B. Anthony is arrested for illegal voting. Anthony had expected to be prevented from voting and then file suit against a person for violating her rights. Because she had been able to cast a ballot, the plan does not work, and no case is brought before the court that could gain women the right to vote.

1876

◆ Southern states begin enacting laws, including the poll tax, grandfather clauses, and literacy tests, that can be used to keep blacks from voting. At this time, the literacy rate is very low in the United States. Poll workers decided who would have to take the literacy test. As a result, blacks are confronted with the test while most whites are not.

1890

◆ *July 10:* Wyoming is admitted to the Union. The new state constitution continues Wyoming women's right to vote, which had been established in Wyoming Territory.

1909

◆ The National Association for the Advancement of Colored People (NAACP) is formed by black and white activists to fight social injustice through the courts.

1920

◆ *August 18:* The Nineteenth Amendment gives women the right to vote. Some states had granted women suffrage before the passage of this amendment. However, women now have universal suffrage, guaranteed by an amendment to the U.S. Constitution that no state may take away.

1924

◆ Congress grants citizenship to Native Americans. Some states, including Maine, Utah, Arizona, and New Mexico, continue to deny the vote to Indians. This legal disenfranchisement of Indians ends in 1962 when New Mexico becomes the final state to abolish state laws used to deny Indians the right to vote.

1964

◆ *January 23:* The Twenty-fourth Amendment abolishes the poll tax. Black and white people who cannot afford to pay the tax before going to the polls finally have the right to vote.

1965

◆ *March 21–25:* Martin Luther King, Jr., leads a civil rights march from Selma, Alabama, to Montgomery, Alabama. The summer of 1965 will be remembered as Freedom Summer.
◆ *August 6:* President Lyndon B. Johnson signs the Civil Rights Act of 1965 after the Freedom Summer voter registration drives attract violent opposition, resulting in bloodshed and death for several workers.

1971

◆ *July 1:* The Twenty-sixth Amendment lowers the voting age to 18. Many people agree that 18-year-olds, who could be sent to war, should be able to elect the government officials who would send them into battle. As a result, the states ratify this amendment quickly.

1975

◆ The Voting Rights Act requires printing voting materials in both minority languages and English to accommodate large numbers of minority groups living in an area.

1993

◆ The National Voter Registration Act, also known as the Motor Voter Act, makes voter registration easier by requiring voter registration opportunities at the Division of Motor Vehicles and public assistance agencies.

2002

◆ *March 27:* President George W. Bush signs the Bipartisan Campaign Reform Act (known as the McCain-Feingold Law). This act is intended to limit corporation and labor union campaign contributions and give more power to individual voters.
◆ *October 22:* The Help America Vote Act (HAVA) requires replacing punch-card voting machines with optical-scan or electronic voting machines. The act also provides money to states for purchasing new voting machines. In addition, HAVA requires accommodating handicapped voters, thus allowing many voters to cast their votes in secret for the first time.

2004

◆ Five hundred twenty-seven nonprofit political organizations bypass the intent of the McCain-Feingold Law. As a result, organizations such as Vietnam Vets for Truth and MoveOn.org play a significant role in the 2004 major party presidential campaigns.

2005

◆ Campaign finance reform remains on the congressional agenda.

Appendix

Excerpts from Documents Relating to the Right to Vote

Constitutional Regulations for Electing the President and Vice President

The Constitution established rules for electing the president and vice president. Problems arose with a tie in the 1800 election. As a result, Congress passed the Twelfth Amendment (ratified in 1804) to prevent the problem from happening again. The Twelfth Amendment overrules Article II, Section 1 of the Constitution:

Each State shall appoint, in such Manner as the Legislature thereof may direct, a Number of Electors, equal to the whole Number of Senators and Representatives to which the State may be entitled in the Congress. . . . The Electors shall meet in their respective States, and vote by Ballot for two Persons, of whom one at least shall not be an Inhabitant of the same State with themselves. And they shall make a List of all the Persons voted for, and of the Number of Votes for each; which List they shall sign and certify, and transmit sealed to the Seat of the Government of the United States, directed to the President of the Senate. The President of the Senate shall, in the Presence of the Senate and House of Representatives, open all the Certificates, and the Votes shall then be counted. The person having the greatest Number of Votes shall be the President, if such Number be a Majority of the whole Number of Electors appointed . . . After the Choice of the President, the Person having the greatest Number of Votes [majority] of the Electors shall be the Vice president.

Source: Section 1, clause 2 & 3, U.S. Constitution, Ratified June 21, 1788.

Congressional Resolution for the First Election

When the U.S. Constitution had been ratified by 11 states, Congress appointed a committee to put the process in motion for electing the first president of the United States. They passed a resolution setting the deadline for ratifying the Constitution that would allow states to be eligible to select electors to participate in the election.

That the first Wednesday in January next, be the day for appointing Electors in the several States, which before the said day shall have ratified the said Constitution, that the first Wednesday in February next, be the day for the Electors to assemble in their respective States, and vote for a President; and that the first Wednesday in March next, be the time, and the present Seat of Congress the place for commencing proceedings under said Constitution.

Source: Second Continental Congress, September 13, 1788.

Constitutional Amendments 1804–1971

TWELFTH AMENDMENT

In the first presidential elections, the nominee receiving the most votes became president and the nominee receiving the second most became vice president. In the 1800 election, however, Democratic-Republican nominees Thomas Jefferson and Aaron Burr received the same number of votes. As a result of the tie, the election was decided in the House of Representatives. To prevent this happening again, Congress proposed the Twelfth Amendment, which determines that president and vice president are elected on separate ballots. This amendment also includes the process for counting the electoral vote.

⤲

The Electors shall meet in their respective states, and vote by ballot for President and Vice-President, one of whom, at least, shall not be an inhabitant of the same state with themselves; they shall name in their ballots the person voted for as President, and in distinct ballots the person voted for as Vice-President, and they shall make distinct lists of all persons voted for as President, and of all persons voted for as Vice-President, and of the number of votes for each, which lists they shall sign and certify, and transmit sealed to the seat of the government of the United States, directed to the President of the Senate;—The President of the Senate shall, in the presence of the Senate and House of Representatives, open all the certificates and the votes shall then be counted;—The person having the greatest number of votes for President, shall be the President, if such number be a majority of the whole number of Electors appointed; and if no person have such majority, then from the persons having the highest numbers not exceeding three on the list of those voted for as President, the House of Representatives shall choose immediately, by ballot, the President. But in choosing the President, the votes shall be taken by states, the representation from each state having one vote; a quorum for this purpose shall consist of a member or members from two-thirds of the states, and a majority of all the states shall be necessary to a choice. And if the House of Representatives shall not choose a President whenever the right of choice shall devolve upon them, before the fourth day of March next following, then the Vice-President shall act as President, as in the case of the death or other constitutional disability of the President. The person having the greatest number of votes as Vice-President, shall be the Vice-President, if such number be a majority of the whole number of Electors appointed, and if no person have a majority, then from the two highest numbers on the list, the Senate shall choose the Vice-President; a quorum for the purpose shall consist of two-thirds of the whole number of Senators, and a majority of the whole number shall be necessary to a choice. But no person constitutionally ineligible to the office of President shall be eligible to that of Vice-President of the United States. Ratified June 15, 1804.

THIRTEENTH AMENDMENT
The Thirteenth Amendment abolishes slavery.

Section 1. Neither slavery nor involuntary servitude, except as a punishment for crime whereof the party shall have been duly convicted, shall exist within the United States, or any place subject to their jurisdiction. Ratified 1865.

FOURTEENTH AMENDMENT
The Fourteenth Amendment makes all people born in the United States, including African Americans, citizens. This amendment also limits the right to vote to male citizens.

Section. 1. All persons born or naturalized in the United States, and subject to the jurisdiction thereof, are citizens of the United States and of the State wherein they reside . . .

Section. 2. Representatives shall be apportioned among the several States according to their respective numbers, counting the whole number of persons in each State, excluding Indians not taxed. But when the right to vote at any election for the choice of electors for President and Vice President of the United States, Representatives in Congress, the Executive and Judicial officers of a State, or the members of the Legislature thereof, is denied to any of the male inhabitants of such State, being twenty-one years of age, and citizens of the United States, or in any way abridged, except for participation in rebellion, or other crime, the basis of representation therein shall be reduced in the proportion which the number of such male citizens shall bear to the whole number of male citizens twenty-one years of age in such State. Ratified 1868.

FIFTEENTH AMENDMENT
The Fifteenth Amendment gives African Americans the right to vote.

The right of citizens of the United States to vote shall not be denied or abridged by the United States or by any State on account of race, color, or previous condition of servitude. Ratified 1870.

SEVENTEENTH AMENDMENT
Until the passage of the Seventeenth Amendment, each state's U.S. senator was appointed by that state's legislature. This amendment

moves the election of U.S. senators from state legislators to a vote of the people.

The Senate of the United States shall be composed of two Senators from each State, elected by the people thereof, for six years; and each Senator shall have one vote. The electors in each State shall have the qualifications requisite for electors of the most numerous branch of the State legislatures. Ratified 1913.

NINETEENTH AMENDMENT
The Nineteenth Amendment gives women the right to vote.

The right of citizens of the United States to vote shall not be denied or abridged by the United States or by any state on account of sex. Ratified 1920.

TWENTY-FOURTH AMENDMENT
This Amendment abolishes the poll tax that was used to keep southern blacks from voting.

The right of citizens of the United States to vote in any primary or other election for President or Vice President, for electors for President or Vice President, or for Senator or Representative in Congress, shall not be denied or abridged by the United States or any State by reason of failure to pay any poll tax or other tax. Ratified 1964.

TWENTY-SIXTH AMENDMENT
This amendment lowers the voting age to 18.

The right of citizens of the United States, who are eighteen years of age or older, to vote shall not be denied or abridged by the United States or by any State on account of age. Ratified 1971.

Source: U.S. Constitution.

Declaration of Sentiments
The women's suffrage movement began in 1848 when a small group of women organized the Women's Convention at Seneca Falls, New

York. They wrote the Declaration of Sentiments, patterned after the Declaration of Independence. In this declaration, the women listed their grievances and the reasons they should have the vote.

When, in the course of human events, it becomes necessary for one portion of the family of man to assume among the people of the earth a position different from that which they have hitherto occupied. . . . We hold these truths to be self-evident: that all men and women are created equal; that they are endowed by their Creator with certain inalienable rights; that among these are life, liberty, and the pursuit of happiness; that to secure these rights governments are instituted, deriving their just powers from the consent of the governed. . . . The history of mankind is a history of repeated injuries and usurpations on the part of man toward woman, having in direct object the establishment of an absolute tyranny over her. To prove this, let facts be submitted to a candid world. He has never permitted her to exercise her inalienable right to the elective franchise. He has compelled her to submit to laws, in the formation of which she had no voice.

He has withheld from her rights which are given to the most ignorant and degraded men—both natives and foreigners. Having deprived her of this first right of a citizen, the elective franchise, thereby leaving her without representation in the halls of legislation, he has oppressed her on all sides. He has made her, if married, in the eye of the law, civilly dead. . . .

Now, in view of this entire disfranchisement of one-half the people of this country . . . women do feel themselves aggrieved, oppressed, and fraudulently deprived of their most sacred rights, we insist that they have immediate admission to all the rights and privileges which belong to them as citizens of the United States.

In entering upon the great work before us, we anticipate no small amount of misconception, misrepresentation, and ridicule; but we shall use every instrumentality within our power to effect our object. We shall employ agents, circulate tracts, petition the State and National legislatures, and endeavor to enlist the pulpit and the press in our behalf. We hope this Convention will be followed by a series of Conventions embracing every part of the country. Firmly relying upon the final triumph of the Right and the True, we do this day affix our signatures to this document.

Source: Declaration of Sentiments, New York, 1848.

Civil Rights Act of 1964

Congress enacted the Civil Rights Act to prevent states from depriving blacks of their right to vote and to outlaw other types of discrimination.

To enforce the constitutional right to vote, to confer jurisdiction upon the district courts of the United States to provide injunctive relief against discrimination in public accommodations, to authorize the attorney General to institute suits to protect constitutional rights in public facilities and public education, to extend the Commission on Civil Rights, to prevent discrimination in federally assisted programs, to establish a Commission on Equal Employment Opportunity, and for other purposes.

Source: Civil Rights Act of 1964.

National Voter Registration Act, 1993

The National Voter Registration Act makes voter registration more accessible: It is available at motor vehicle departments and government offices that provide public assistance.

Provisions of the National Voter Registration Act: Motor Voter Registration allows voters to register to vote at the Department of Motor Vehicles when they apply for a driver's license or register a vehicle. Agency-based Voter Registration requires offering voter registration and assistance to each applicant for services, service renewal or address change through all offices that provide public assistance and all offices that provide state-funded programs primarily engaged in providing services to persons with disabilities.

Source: U.S. Department of Justice.

Help America Vote Act, 2002

Congress passed this act to address the many problems in the 2000 presidential election that resulted from the punch-card voting machines. The act requires that states change voting systems and set standards for the administration of elections. The act also provides money for the purchase of new voting equipment.

An Act to establish a program to provide funds to States to replace punch card voting systems, to establish the Election Assistance Commission to assist in the administration of Federal elections and to otherwise provide assistance with the administration of certain Federal election law and programs, to establish minimum election administration standards for States and units of local government with responsibility for the administration of Federal elections, and for other purposes.

Source: Help America Vote Act, 2002.

Further Reading

Books

Bausum, Ann. *With Courage and Cloth: How American Women Fought for and Won the Right to Vote.* Washington, D.C.: National Geographic, 2004.

Collier, Christopher, and James Lincoln Collier. *Reconstruction and the Rise of Jim Crow: 1864–1896.* New York: Benchmark Books, 2000.

Freedman, Russell. *In Defense of Liberty: The Story of America's Bill of Rights.* New York: Holiday House, 2003.

Kielburger, Marc, and Craig Kielburger. *Take Action! A Guide to Active Citizenship.* Hoboken, N.J.: John Wiley & Sons, 2002.

Litwin, Laura Baskes. *Fannie Lou Hamer: Fighting for the Right to Vote.* Berkeley Heights, N.J.: Enslow Publishers, 2002.

Web Sites

"Ben's Guide to U.S. Government for Kids Grade 9–12," U.S. Government Printing Office Web site. Available online. URL: http://bensguide.gpo.gov/9-12/index.html. Updated May 4, 2001.

Burton, David L. "How to Detect Bias," Outreach Missouri Web site. Available online. URL: http://outreach.missouri.edu/swregion/news/Publications/How%2OTo%20Detect%20Bias.pdf. Downloaded June 1, 2004.

"Can You Explain the Presidential Nomination Process? How Does the Delegate System Work?" Questions & Answers Archive. This Nation Web site. Available online. URL: http://www.thisnation.com/question/print/021p.html. Downloaded January 21, 2004.

Feldman, Ruth Tenzer. "The Scoop on the Media and Elections," Cobblestone Elections in America Issue. Cobblestone Publishing Web site. Available online. URL: http://www.cobblestonepub.com/pages/FACOBElections.html. Posted in October 1996.

Pitts, David. "Mississippi Freedom Summer Remembered," U.S. Department of State International Information Programs Web site. Available online. URL: http://usinfo.state.gov/usa/blackhis/missis.htm. Updated May 2, 2001.

Project Vote Smart Web site. Available online. URL: http://www.vote-smart.org. Downloaded May 19, 2004.

Bibliography

Books

Altschuler, Glenn C. *Rude Republic: Americans and Their Politics in the Nineteenth Century.* Princeton, N.J.: Princeton University Press, 2000.

Durr, Virginia Foster. *Outside the Magic Circle.* Tuscaloosa: University of Alabama Press, 1990.

Ellis, Joseph J. *Founding Brothers: The Revolutionary Generation.* New York: Alfred A. Knopf, 2001.

Jamieson, Kathleen Hall. *Packaging the Presidency: A History and Criticism of Presidential Campaign Advertising.* New York: Oxford University Press, 1996.

Keyssar, Alexander. *The Right to Vote: The Contested History of Democracy in the United States.* New York: Basic Books, 2000.

Lossing, Benson J. *Our Country: Volume 3.* New York: Lossing History Company, 1905.

Miller, Zell. *A National Party No More: The Conscience of a Conservative Democrat.* Atlanta, Ga.: Stroud & Hall Publishing, 2003.

Web Sites

"About Elections and Voting," Federal Elections Commission. Available online. URL: http://fecwebl.fec.gov/elections.html. Downloaded May 12, 2004.

"About the Declaration of Independence," Thomas, Library of Congress. Available online. URL: http://memory.loc.gov/const/abt_declar.html. Updated May 31, 1996.

Baker, Brent. "NPR's Williams Sees No Liberal Bias, *NYT 'Mainstream Journalism,'*" June 1, 2004. Media Research Center. Available online. URL: http://www.mediaresearch.org/cyberalerts/2004/cyb20040601.asp#4. Downloaded June 1, 2004.

"Campaigning," The Presidential Elections 1860–1912. Harpweek Exploring History. Available online. URL: http://elections.harpweek.com/NewSite/Campaigning-l.htm. Downloaded May 21, 2004.

A Century of Lawmaking for a New Nation: U.S. Congressional Documents and Debates, 1774–1875. "Journal of the continental Congress, Volume 32, pages 71–74," American Memory, Library of Congress. Available online. URL: http://memory.loc.gov/cgi-bin/ampage?collId=lljc&fileName=032/lljcO32.db&recNum=80. Downloaded May 12, 2004.

"Citizenship: A Challenge for All Generations," National Conference of State Legislatures. Available online. URL: www.ncsl.org/public/trust/citizenship.pdf. September 2003.

"Civics," The Nation's Report Card. National Center for Education Statistics. Available online. URL: http://nces.ed.gov/nationsreportcard/civics. Downloaded May 13, 2004.

Continental Congress & Constitutional Convention. "To Form a More Perfect Union: The Work of the Continental Congress and the Constitutional Convention," Rare Book and Special Collections Division, Library of Congress. Available online. URL: http://memory.loc.gov/ammem/bdsds/intro0l.html. Downloaded May 8, 2004.

"From Revolution to Reconstruction . . . and What Happened Afterwards," Department of Humanities Computing, University of Groningen, The Netherlands. Available online. URL: http://odur.let.rug.nl/~usa/. Downloaded May 8, 2004.

Gilder Lehrman Center for the Study of Slavery, Resistance, and Abolition. "Jim Crow Laws," The Code of Alabama, v.1.1923. Atlanta. Yale Center for International and Area Studies. Available online. URL: http://www.yale.edu/glc/archive/976.htm. Downloaded May 13, 2004.

Hamilton, Alexander. Federalist No. 68. History Central. Available online. URL: http://www.multied.com/elections/Federalist.html. Downloaded January 23, 2004.

Henry, Patrick. "Give Me Liberty or Give Me Death," University of Oklahoma Law Center. Available online. URL: http://www.law.ou.edu/hist/henry.html. Downloaded May 12, 2004.

Kimberling, William C. "The Electoral College," About Elections and Voting, Federal Election Commission. Available online. URL: http://www.fec.gov/pdf/eleccoll.pdf. Downloaded May 19, 2004.

League of Women Voters. "Alienation Not a Factor in Nonvoting," Publications: Representative Government, Barbara Stuhler E-Library. Available online. URL: http://www.lwv.org/elibrary/pub/mellman.htm. Downloaded April 19, 2004.

Linder, Doug. "The Trial of Susan B. Anthony for Illegal Voting," Famous Trials. University of Missouri Kansas City School of Law. Available online. URL: http://www.law.umkc.edu/faculty/projects/ftrials/anthony/sbaaccount.html. Downloaded September 15, 2003.

National American Women Suffrage Association Collection Home Page. "Votes for Women: Timeline." Rare Book and Special Collections Division, Library of Congress. Available online. URL: http://memory.loc.gov/ammem/naw/nawstime.html. October 19, 1988.

"Native American Citizenship," Nebraska Studies. Available online. URL:http://www.nebraskastudies.org/0700/stories/0701_0141.html. Downloaded May 17, 2004.

Roberts, Cokie. "One Journalist's View: Informed Voters Must Reach Beyond Images," Center for Media Literacy. Available online. URL: http://www.medialit.org/reading_room/article397.html. Downloaded May 21, 2004.

Rosen, Jay. "PressThink's Questions and Answers about Media Bias," New York University. Available online. URL: http://journalism.nyu.edu/pubzone/weblogs/pressthink/2004/05/22/qa_bias.html. Downloaded May 22, 2004.

Smith, Marian L. "Overview of INS History," Bureau of Citizenship and Immigration Services. Available online. URL: http://uscis.gov/graphics/aboutus/history/articles/OVIEW.htm. Updated February 28, 2003.

Stanton, Elizabeth Cady. "Address: First Women's Rights Convention," July 19, 1848. Institute for the Study of Civic Values. Liberty Net. Available online. URL: http://www.libertynet.org/edcivic/stanton.html.

"The Right to Vote: How Federal Law Protects You," Civil Rights Division, U.S. Department of Justice. Available online. URL: http://www.usdoj.gov/crt/voting/misc/voterev.htm. Updated February 4, 2003.

U.S. Constitution Online. USConstitution.net. Available online. URL: http://www.usconstitution.net/const.html. Downloaded May 7, 2004.

"Use of Internet in Presidential Campaigns, Lessons of 2000 Race Analyzed in Book by UC Santa Barbara Political Scientist," University of California, Santa Barbara. November 18, 2003. Available online. URL: http://www.ia.ucsb.edu/release/Display.aspx?PKey=1060. Accessed March 17, 2005.

Voting Section Home Page, Civil Rights Division, United States Department of Justice. Available online. URL: http://www.usdoj.gov/crt/voting/. Updated May 11, 2004.

Wayne, Leslie. "E-mail Used to Mobilize Voters," Technology, *New York Times*. November 6, 2000. Available online. URL: http://www.nytimes.com/2000/11/06/technology/06MAIL.html?ex=1085284800&en=6e8ae683-c91a9820&el=5070. Downloaded March 21, 2005.

Index

Page numbers in *italic* indicate photographs. Page numbers in **boldface** indicate box features and margin quotations. Page numbers followed by *m* indicate maps. Page numbers followed by *t* indicate tables or graphs. Page numbers followed by *g* indicate glossary entries. Page numbers followed by *c* indicate chronology entries.